1   A history of privacy

Early days

It might be argued that privacy and private space are natural needs for people and even animals. As birds spread out along a telephone wire, so cats and dogs mark out their territorial claims on the ground. The ancient Greeks, on the other hand, regarded participation in the communal world as equally natural, and a life spent in the privacy of 'one's own' (*idion*) was, by definition, 'idiotic'. Not to be a part of the public realm was to live a lesser form of life, and to be a 'private' person was literally to live a life of 'deprivation' (Wacks 1989, p. 7).

Privacy in pre-industrial times and in primitive societies could be a remote possibility in the communal world of the village or small town:

> Villagers and town dwellers alike knew most of the others they were ever likely to meet, because they had ample opportunity to watch them – to watch continuously, in all their functions and on most diverse occasions. Theirs were communities perpetuated and reproduced by mutual watching. (Bauman 1987, p. 39)

If people were not watching each other, then God was watching, even when you thought you were alone: 'The metaphor is that of the small craftsman in his workshop, "forever in my great Taskmaster's eye"' (Hill 1970, p. 243). If this was a form of surveillance, it was being carried out within a spirit of reciprocity. The watchers one day could be the watched the next. A degree of symmetry was present. This public life of the small-scale society has usually been contrasted with that of the privatised anonymity typified by modern society. Recent findings suggest this is not an absolute rule, and some primitive societies have been found to have very sophisticated rituals to ensure privacy and confidentiality in their every-day activities (see, for example, Haviland and Haviland 1983).

Sennett tells us that the first use of the word 'public' as opposed to 'private' was to distinguish the common good in society (public) from other activities (Sennett 1977, p. 16). 'Private' at this time was also used to refer to the more privileged way of life of those in positions of power, and ultimately to refer to that which was privately owned and which people would expect to hold against 'trespassers' and other 'nuisances'. Beset by more and more people coming in and new buildings and streets being built, this 'small and stable, and hence tightly controlled world of the pre-modern man came under heavy stress in the sixteenth century, to be irretrievably shattered in the next' (Bauman 1987, p. 40).

In historical terms, privacy and the right to a private life also came to be seen as a way in which a governed people could ensure a degree of protection for themselves against those who govern, either as monarch or constitutionally elected parliament. Just as those who govern may require a degree of privacy surrounding their activities in the interests of state security, so the people of that State should be able to safeguard an area of life for themselves in the interests of 'balanced' government.

The concept of the king's or queen's 'peace' developed, and a person's home and family life took on aspects of that 'peace' which should not be disturbed: 'The peace of the King was originally the peace of the householder writ large' (Feldman 1993, p. 381). The king's courts – and later, police forces – would ensure a peace wherein people could act with freedom, free from public nuisance and breaches of the peace. Even today, all new police officers swear, first and foremost, to 'cause the peace to be kept and preserved' (Police Act 1964, Schedule 2). In such a climate, 'the house of everyone is to him as his castle and fortress, as well for his defence against injury and violence as for his repose' (*Semayne's case*, 1604, 5 Co. Rep. 91a at 91b). Alternatively, an Englishman's home was his castle – and, for many, still is today – complete with the gender-specific connotations of the phrase. Such notions of private space, however, depended more on the overall freedom of people that was being nurtured, rather than any concept of a right to privacy: a freedom from governmental intrusion, and the development of a free civil society – if necessary, in healthy opposition to centrally-held state powers. Within such a civil society, the value of – if not the right to – privacy could grow and become a central tenet of civil liberties. If the 'dense sociability' of pre-modern times helped form the small communal identity with self-regulatory forms of social control involving everyone watching everyone else, it also created the notion of people outside that community being defined as somehow 'the other' or even 'the enemy'. You were either part of that society or you were not.

As industrialism progressed and people moved – or were evicted – from the countryside to the new cities, a new phenomenon arose. This was the concept of 'the stranger'. Life could no longer be broken down into simple divisions of 'insiders' and 'outsiders' – here was a new person living alongside you who was difficult to classify. New forms of identification would be needed to help make judgements on the stranger's deviance or conformity, to reduce the idea of the stranger as some sort of 'threat'.

At the same time, the growth of the market economy to replace the feudal economy, coupled with the growth of cities and population, led to a realignment of thinking on the 'private' and the 'public'. The new individualism led to private property, the private ownership of the means of production, and new ideas on the notion of a private life. Replacing the 'watchful' village with the 'city of strangers' required more sophisticated symbols and systems to allow identification and make the city work. The State had to move into the gap left when old-style forms of community control broke down. Some of this new thinking was incorporated into overt systems of social control. The new cities were not particularly safe places, and crime and 'danger' were endemic. The Victorians would later refer to whole sections of society as the 'dangerous classes'. Many urban public areas where once you could 'promenade' in safety became places you moved through as fast as possible as you moved from one private area to another (Sennett 1977).

In our own times, increasing interest has been shown in one social control model first put forward in 1791. This is the idea of the 'panopticon', proposed as a design for a prison by Jeremy Bentham. Bentham's plans never came to fruition, but elements of the 'panopticon' idea passed into general currency and offered a framework for organising society on safer lines (Foucault 1977; Ignatieff 1978; Lyon 1994). In the original plan, both prisoner and guard alike were under constant surveillance – the prisoners by the guards, the guards by a central inspector. The central inspector was overseen by members of the public, given free admission to a specially-built inspection tower. It was the creation of a society where everyone watched everyone else in a state of 'omnipresent inspection' (Ignatieff 1978, p. 78). In truth, it was the embodiment of 'the eye of the state – impartial, humane and vigilant – holding the "deviant" in the thrall of its omniscient gaze' (Ignatieff 1978, p. 113). Unlike the reciprocal watching of earlier societies, the new surveillance was strictly asymmetrical, with people in power watching over those without.

Whilst the nineteenth-century 'social engineers' started looking at the macro-problems, the individual was left to look after him or her self. Escaping from the dangers of the city involved retiring to the privacy of your family and household. Here you were away from government interference, criminals, violence and danger. The home became the haven in a heartless world. In practice, the private–public division was never so clear-cut and was always the subject of contention, as it is today. The rise of the privately-owned 'public house', for example, epitomised the ambiguity: it remained 'public' for purposes of law enforcement if the public got drunk and disorderly. Alongside the 'public house' were the now forgotten coffee-house and the first restaurants and men's clubs. As Sennett records:

> As information centres, the coffeehouses naturally were places in which speech flourished ... [and] for information to be as full as possible, distinctions of rank were temporarily suspended; any one sitting in the coffee house had a right to talk to any one else. (Sennett 1977, p. 81).

The private–public division was also being drawn differently by men and women. From an earlier age of rural life and domestic cottage industry, the new industrialisation required new disciplines of time-keeping and being in particular places at particular times. At first its labour-force was drawn indiscriminately from men, women and children, but in time the regulation of the workplace tended towards the creation of a largely male work-force as producers. The role of women and children was re-drawn into one of domesticity, to maintain the home and the private areas of life, and to be 're-producers'. The public domain slowly became the domain of men – men in the workplace and men in civic and public life, whilst women looked after the 'haven in a heartless world' for the men to return to. A 'man of the world' could cope with the harsher disciplines of working life, understand and use the liberated market forces and move into a political public life where women, at first, would not even have a vote. Men could also better cope with the dangers of the street and the drunkenness of the 'public house'. Women seen in the 'wrong' place risked the negative inflexions of being called 'a woman of the world', or even 'a woman of the night'.

The policing of dangerous public areas had to be re-thought. Where once there had been self-regulation in the small community through mutual surveillance, there now developed the idea of the night-watch: people paid by private enterprise – and, later, civic authorities – to ensure someone was watching over public space on behalf of everyone. This saw the idea of the 'panopticon' taken into the community. The idea of 'justice' became abstracted from the community, and the police sought evidence of wrong-doing to present before this abstracted concept. To symbolise her (sic) removal from the community and any degree of watching, justice not only retreated but carried scales and put on a blindfold to demonstrate she herself was not a part of the watching society but would listen impartially to evidence put before her.

This picture is, of necessity, a simplified sketch. Public and private related to each other in complex, dynamic ways, sometimes contradictory, and often ambiguous. Women did remain in the workplace in, for example, the mills of Lancashire and Yorkshire. A public area of town could even change in nature during the course of the day, meaning that women who walked there in the afternoon might be ill-advised to do so in the evening. In general terms, men became adept at existing in the public world, whilst women were confined to the private. Each developed a different awareness of the community they lived in, with men leaving it behind to travel to work, returning only in the evenings and for weekends, and women being a constant presence and having a different spatial awareness of the community, viewed from their private domain.

The late nineteenth and early twentieth centuries also saw the rise of the administrative role within society. Based on the idea of the 'bureau' the phenomenon of 'bureaucracy' as a new departure in organising society was most famously dissected by Max Weber. Eventually, bureaucracy would become the natural home for policing, welfare and other surveillance programmes charged with improving on the 'natural' state of free-market societies. The essential characteristics of bureaucracy were its ability to get jobs done by forming people into a hierarchy, with each person having a specific role, developing a body of expertise and carrying out roles in an impersonal, rational manner, following given rules. The impersonal treatment of 'cases' meant standardised services which had a degree of continuity, as the bureaucracy simply replaced its workers to carry on the same job as and when required. Individuality in delivering services was deliberately repressed.

The full political and economic consequences of the rise of bureaucracy are beyond the scope of this book, and the reader is referred elsewhere for discussion of this (see, for example, Beetham 1987). What we can note is the importance attached to dealing with 'cases' on a rational basis, and to that end, the centrality of the 'case-file' to the bureaucracy in order to standardise and offer continuity of service. We might also note the influence of the ordered and routine approach of the bureaucracy in its dealings with the world as a set of values that would become influential beyond the confines of the bureaucracy:

> Instrumental values would come to prevail in society at large ... In particular the values of order and security, nurtured in a bureaucratic environment, in which everything was precisely regulated would come to prevail over the innovative, risk taking approach of the industrial entrepreneur or political leader. (Beetham 1987, p. 61)

Ultimately, the bureaucracy would be resisted in order to keep people free from its ordered ideal and excessive 'red tape'.

Within the welfare world, one of the first agencies to marry charity with bureaucracy was the Charity Organisation Society (COS), founded in 1869. The COS was conscious that charity was being given by one sector of society to another sector that it did not know. According to its founder, C.S. Loch: 'In a great city the larger proportion of applicants for relief are made from strangers to strangers' (cited in Fido 1977). In order to put charity on an organised, formal footing, the COS sought to record as much information as possible about a person and family before giving them charity.

Bureaucracy was also attuned to help the creation of a national collection of criminal records. Designed to keep track of offenders no longer transported to Australia or so readily executed by hanging, the criminal record system came into being in the 1870s. It was also a response to the inefficient system of granting and revoking licences to ex-prisoners – the so-called 'ticket-of-leave men' – such that in 1862, when the Home Office asked the Commissioner of the Metropolitan Police to report on 'ticket-of-leave men', the commissioner was compelled to admit 'the police could not find or produce a single man of them' (Radzinowicz and Hood 1990, p. 249).

Twentieth-century developments

Despite the apparent division on gender lines, it was the men in the public sphere who first tried to define privacy in a more formal sense. Lawyers in the USA have been attributed as being the first to recognise the legal importance of privacy. Their concern was that men in the public sphere should still have an entitlement to an area of life that could be recognised as private. Warren and Brandeis's seminal article declared:

> The intensity and complexity of life, antecedent upon advancing civilisation, have rendered necessary some retreat from the world, and man, under the refining influence of culture, has become more sensitive to publicity so that solitude and privacy have become more essential to the individual. (Warren and Brandeis 1890, p. 196)

For the North Americans, this right to be let alone required legal protection in the form of a tort of 'invasion of privacy' and, ultimately, privacy laws. The UK courts took no such parallel course, preferring the defence of liberty rather than the creation of a legal right to privacy.

Apart from legalities, privacy was also being recognised as something which would enhance the individual's sense of well-being. As people in the sixteenth century had recognised a need for privacy from monarch and State in civil society to safeguard their collective autonomy from oppressive law-makers, privacy was re-formulated on the verge of the twentieth century as something that would enhance each individual's psychological sense of self and autonomy: an area of life reserved for intimate thoughts and behaviour, away from the view of the public domain.

Such an analysis tends toward an assumption that the individual requiring privacy was a man, and tends to overlook the fact that most men were
living in family or household units. Women living in a permanent private
zone of life were presumably deemed to be less in need of additional
safeguards on privacy. It also overlooks the possibility that privacy, although encouraging a sense of self and autonomy for men normally bound
up in the disciplines of the public world, also allowed those same men to be
free of public disciplines in less positive ways. Privacy gave free rein to
patriarchal attitudes and other anti-social acts towards other members of
the household in the belief that here was an area free from public restraint
and where the Englishman's home was indeed still his castle. For some
women and children the home was far from being a 'haven in a heartless
world'.

With a legal and psychological need for privacy having been established,
attention now turned to a political claim for privacy. In the 1930s the restrictions placed on civil societies in Fascist Germany and the Communist So-
viet Union brought a new awareness of the need to define privacy and civil
liberties generally. For the Nazis, 'the only person who is still a private
individual in Germany is somebody who is asleep', and Lenin had gone on
record in the USSR as saying: 'We recognise nothing private. Our morality
is entirely subordinate to the interests of the class struggle of the prole-
tariat' (both cited in Lyon 1994, pp. 185–6).

The writings of Franz Kafka also depicted a world in which people were
living in perpetual uncertainty in the face of invisible bureaucrats who held
certainty for themselves alone, and a society where people were constantly
to be judged and asked to identify themselves and justify their actions,
sometimes without even knowing the charge that had put them on trial.
The phrase 'Kafkaesque' slipped into the English language.

In 1934 the UK National Council of Civil Liberties was founded, and the
prophetic writings of George Orwell warned of what would happen when
communal life became all-pervading to the exclusion of any private life.
Ultimately, we would all look back with nostalgia: 'to a time when there
was still privacy, love and friendship, and when the members of a family
stood by one another without needing to know the reason' (Orwell 1949).
The West, through various inter-governmental organisations, placed on
record its concern for the human rights which seemed to be at risk as a
result of the direction certain countries were taking. Only with the fall of
Nazi Germany, and much later, of Communism in the late 1980s, was the
extent of the loss of that privacy revealed (see, for example, Bridge 1992).
On the question of privacy, the United Nations *Universal Declaration of
Human Rights* made it quite clear that: 'No one shall be subjected to arbi-
trary interference with his privacy, family, home or correspondence' (United
Nations 1948, Article 12). The newly-formed Council of Europe followed up

with its own *Convention on Human Rights*, which required all its member states to ensure: 'Everyone has the right to respect for his private and family life, his home and his correspondence' (Council of Europe 1950, Article 8). Both offer clear political statements on the value of privacy. The later 1966 International Covenant on Civil and Political Rights (Article 17) sought to reinforce the UN's Universal Declaration using identical wording and placing the declaration in Specific Treaty Law (see Michael 1994, Chapter 2); in 1989 the European Parliament passed its own Declaration of Fundamental Rights and Freedoms (*Official Journal of the European Communities*, C120, 16 May 1989, pp. 51–7).

The boundaries between the psychological, political and legal dimensions are not always clear. As a need for privacy arises (psychological), it may be interpreted as a civil right in various ways (political) and finally claimed as a legal right in law (legal).

During the 1960s, in Western Europe and the USA, new developments in technology combined with social changes to create a new awareness of both privacy and information privacy. The new information technologies of the early computers, allied to bureaucracy, were quickly recognised as being capable of storing personal information on a scale never before seen and retrieving that information at frighteningly high speed. The new word 'data' moved into the language, describing the information now stored, to be quickly followed by the need for individuals to be given 'protection' from this new scale of operations. The German state of Hesse has been attributed as being the first government office to recognise the need for a data protection commissioner, in 1970 (Bennett 1992, p. 48).

Information had been kept by public bureaucracies in a pre-computer age, but as it was mostly benign information or connected to crime control, no one really bothered too much about it. The new urban developments and the greater mobility of populations had led to police in Western Europe and the USA building up national criminal record systems in order to keep track of known criminals and help discover if they were responsible for new crimes committed after their sentences had been served. In the UK, as we have seen, the ending of prisoner transportation and the growing acceptance that prisoners would come back into the community and not disappear to the other side of the world – or be executed – also prompted the need for new information systems (see Hebenton and Thomas 1993). As long as criminals were somehow a class apart, little concern was expressed as these record systems developed into the twentieth century. More concern was expressed when middle-class people found themselves swept up into their machinations.

On both sides of the Atlantic, middle-class car-owners in the post-war period began to find themselves entangled with law enforcement officers in ways they had not experienced before. Traffic offences for speeding or licence evasion drew them firstly into an awareness of police powers, and secondly, their ability to store personal information regarding people. By the 1960s this information would be finding its way onto computer data banks.

The late 1960s also saw a wave of political protests sweeping the Western world, from those opposed to the Vietnam War through to the university 'sit-ins' of 1968 across Europe. The intensity and effectiveness of these protests, demonstrations and other forms of direct action may be debated, but from our point of view, they again entangled middle-class people with the agents of law enforcement and again sensitised people to the police powers to collate and keep personal information on the populace. The United Nations declared 1968 as Human Rights Year. *Nineteen Eighty-Four* was beginning to make sense, and not just in Eastern Europe and the USSR.

The issue was spelt out in graphic terms in the USA during debate in the Senate prior to the enactment of the Privacy Act 1974:

> in the past, dictatorships always have come with hobnailed boots and tanks and machine guns, but a dictatorship of dossiers, a dictatorship of data banks can be just as repressive, just as chilling and just as debilitating. (cited in Stallworthy 1990)

And the same point was made later by Cohen, in his oft-quoted belief that:

> Orwell's terrible image of totalitarianism was the boot externally trampling a human face. My vision of social control is much more mundane and assuring. It is the eternal case conference ... studying the same computerised records, psychological profiles, case histories, neat files punched out on the word processor. (Cohen 1985, p. 185)

In the UK a private member's bill was introduced by Lord Mancroft in 1961. It was to be the first of many unsuccessful bills to try to regulate privacy. In 1967 the International Commission of Jurists held the Nordic Conference on the Right of Privacy in Stockholm, and prompted JUSTICE, the UK section of the commission, to produce its own report on the subject (JUSTICE 1970). Using the JUSTICE report as a model, Brian Walden MP made another attempt to bring in a private member's bill in 1970. This flurry of activity prompted the government to set up a committee under the chairmanship of Kenneth Younger to look into the problem.

The Younger Report was limited by only focusing on the private sector and not the public, and by not looking at police activities. It tried to formulate a definition of privacy, but like many before, and after, had to admit: 'the concept of privacy cannot be satisfactorily defined' (Younger Report 1972, para. 58). Definitions apart, however, Younger did confirm the importance people attached to privacy, and although it might vary in time and place and between individuals, and therefore constitute a rather incoherent concept, it remained true that: 'privacy is a basic need, essential to the development and maintenance both of a free society and of a mature and stable individual personality' (para. 113).

The Younger Report also opened up the distinction between privacy and information privacy. The distinction had been made elsewhere, most notably by Westin in the USA (Westin 1967). Although a legal right to privacy might not be possible, and was not recommended by Younger, a legal right to information privacy was a more realistic idea. The government responded by asking the Law Commission to look at the law on breach of confidence (see Law Commission 1981) and by turning its attention to computer-held information. Two White Papers on this subject appeared in the mid-1970s, but did not take the arguments much further forward (Home Office 1975a and 1975b). Instead, another committee, chaired by Sir Norman Lindop, was established to look solely at information privacy with respect to computers.

The resulting Lindop Report again struggled with the idea of defining privacy, and ultimately shared the view of the Younger Committee that no useful purpose was served by trying to define it (Lindop Report 1978, para. 2.01). Even on the more secure grounds of private information or data, it was hard to formulate definitions because there is 'wide variation in what data about themselves people regard as private' (para. 2.05). The Lindop Report was not immediately acted upon, and it was only after a change of government and the promptings of the international community in the shape of the Council of Europe that the UK government enacted legislation to regulate the use of personal information held on computers.

It could be said that from the 1970s through to the present day, privacy and data protection has had a higher profile at an international level of politics than it has at domestic levels. Where important economic and political interests are at stake over trans-border data flows, the international community has responded more vigorously than the relatively low-key response of national governments (Raab and Bennett 1994).

The Council of Europe's convention on data protection required all its member states to put national data protection legislation in place (Council of Europe 1980). Many had already done so. Austria, Denmark, France, Germany, Luxemburg, Norway and Sweden had all legislated in the 1970s. Now the UK responded with its Data Protection Act 1984. The Republic of Ireland introduced its own Data Protection Act in 1988, and other countries similarly fell into line. Germany produced its second Data Protection Act in 1990 to take account of re-unification between East and West. Other countries lagged behind – Belgium, Greece and Italy, for example – and dragged their heels on introducing legislation. The Council of Europe convention covered automated and non-automated data (Article 2), and although some countries legislated for both, the UK chose to leave non-automated manual files to one side and pass a law on computer-held information only.

In 1990, in order to prompt some of its own member states into action, the European Commission published a draft Directive on Data Protection that would apply to all EC countries. The commission took a general approach to data protection, applying common principles to all sectors, rather than the sectoral approach of the Council of Europe. The aim was to have the draft directive (reference COM(90) 314 Final SYN 287) enacted before 1 January 1993, when the EC's frontiers would be opened. This deadline proved impossible, and criticisms of the draft directive were received from a number of quarters, including an opinion from the European Parliament. UK critics disliked the extension of jurisdiction to manual files and the distinction being made between the public and private sectors (see House of Commons 1991). A revised draft was issued in 1992 (reference COM(92) 422 Final SYN 287), and at the time of writing was still being considered by ministers and civil servants at the Home Office and other concerned government departments.

Privacy

As attention has turned to the more easily regulated information privacy, what has become of our thoughts on privacy? As we noted, this is a much more difficult concept to pin down:

> everyone needs some privacy ... some need more than others ... the more you have the more you cherish it ... deprivation of privacy can be harmful, but so too can excess of it and ... the effects of both vary from person to person. (Younger Report 1972, para. 105)

We may feel it is easier to decide when our privacy has been invaded or intruded upon, rather than drawing a definitive zone of privacy around us. Some are, by inclination, more 'public figures' than others, who may prefer the role of private citizen. A need for privacy varies in one person over time and in different situations. The footballer enjoys the adulation of the crowd one minute, and after his simple error, wishes the ground would open up and swallow him the next.

The Calcutt Committee, reporting in 1990 on press intrusions into privacy, had been established after concerns that the tabloid press in the UK were over-stepping the mark in terms of stories published about the private lives of public figures. The Calcutt Committee accepted that there was 'little possibility of producing a precise or exhaustive definition of privacy' (Home Office 1990a, para. 3.4), and could only resort to listing items they considered the antithesis of what is public as constituting what is private. In this way, 'privacy could be regarded as ... everything concerning an individual's home, family, religion, health, sexuality, personal legal and personal financial affairs' (para. 3.5).

At present, the UK still has no law comparable to say the US Privacy Act 1974, or the French legislation of 1970 which provides that each person has the 'rights to one's personality' ('les droits de la personnalité'). When the Court of Appeal granted injunctions restraining the publication of press interviews with a well-known actor, it had cause to dwell on the lack of a right to privacy in English law. The actor was recovering from brain surgery in a hospital when journalists tracked him down to his cubicle. Lord Justice Bingham was moved to say that, if ever a person had a right to privacy, it must surely be when he lies in hospital recovering from surgery and in only partial command of his faculties. Unfortunately, English law did not entitle him to relief for that gross invasion of privacy (*Kaye* v. *Robertson* [1991] FSR 62 CA).

Concern has also been expressed that a person's privacy might be invaded in a public area by people who follow them around in a form of 'stalking'. At present the law fails to offer adequate protection, although there is limited help from the Conspiracy and Protection of Property Act 1875, Section 7. That Act is more directed at intervention in industrial relations disputes, and 'stalking' in other situations remains an area of uncertainty for the police (see also Turl 1994).

One aspect of privacy is guarded by the laws of trespass and nuisance. Both are dependent on ownership of land or property, but in practice they do provide a degree of seclusion that we might equate with privacy. A trespasser can be removed from land or premises, using reasonable force if necessary. However, neither the torts of trespass to land or nuisance can be said to amount to a right to privacy, and they might still be said to protect property rather than privacy. There is no general criminal offence of trespass to land, but the Criminal Justice and Public Order Act 1994 does make it a criminal offence to ignore a police direction to leave a given space of land (Section 61) or to fail to leave specified residential premises that have been entered violently if asked to do so by the 'proper' occupier (Sections 72–3).

References to 'privacy' and 'private' areas crop up occasionally in the statutory law, but often without a clear definition of what is meant. The Mental Health Act 1983, for example, says doctors must interview patients in 'private' in certain circumstances (Section 24(1)), and the law legalising homosexual activity in the UK allows it only in 'private' (Sexual Offences Act 1967, Section 1; see also Liberty 1994a, pp. 46–8).

Whilst a legal definition of privacy remains problematic, perhaps a definitive definition on psychological or philosophical grounds is less important. It could be argued that other values, like 'equality', 'freedom' and 'liberty', are equally difficult to pin down. Perhaps of more importance is the value we generally place on privacy. For one observer of privacy, there is no doubt that privacy 'is one of the truly profound values for a civilised society ... privacy is surely deeply linked to individual dignity and the needs of human existence' (cited in Lord Chancellor's Department 1993, p. 10). Surveys of public opinion appear to bear this statement out.

The Younger Report carried out a survey of attitudes to privacy and concluded that 'privacy is undoubtedly of consequence to many, and possibly most people' (Younger Report 1972, para. 103). The Data Protection Registrar takes an annual sounding of public opinion which consistently rates 'privacy' high as an important issue amongst other public issues (DPR 1994, Appendix 5), and a Gallup survey in 1992 found 87 per cent of those questioned favoured the introduction of statutory rights to privacy ('Survey indicates support for law on privacy', *The Independent*, 8 August 1992).

With most people placing a high value on privacy and few wishing to lose their privacy, the definition only returns to haunt us in the strictly legal sense. One way forward has been to focus on information privacy rather than a wider idea of privacy.

Information privacy

The difficulties of defining privacy do not stop people valuing it, making political declarations on a right to privacy, and trying to define it in legal terms. But a number of commentators have asked us to turn our attention away from 'privacy' to the more fruitful concept of 'information privacy'. The extent of information privacy is measured by the ability we have to control the amount of personal information about us that circulates in society:

> Instead of pursuing the false god of 'privacy', attention should be paid to identifying what specific interests of the individual we think the law ought to protect. And it is submitted that at the core of the preoccupation with the 'right to privacy' is the protection against the misuse of personal, sensitive information. (Wacks 1989, p. 10)

Similarly, Westin, from an earlier age, in his ground-breaking work stated:

> the first way we can try to come to grips with [the problem of loss of 'privacy'] is to develop a new way of classifying information to identify what is private and 'non-circulating'; what is confidential, with limited circulation; and what is public and freely circulating. This can also be seen as a distinction between the facts about ourselves that are intimate; those that are part of our life transactions

(education, employment, family etc.) and those that are formal public records. (Westin 1967, p. 322)

The Younger Report felt that a wide interpretation of privacy as being a state of being 'let alone' was too broad to be meaningful (Younger Report 1972, paras. 62–3). A process of narrowing down, however, found most concerns were expressed when 'invasion of privacy involves the treatment of personal information' (para. 64).

If 'privacy' is too amorphous and incoherent a concept, 'information privacy' offers more definite hope of political and legal definition; it is also held in equal esteem by most people. We have already made mention of the Data Protection Registrar's research into public attitudes to privacy (DPR 1994, Appendix 5). On the basis of his research, he told the House of Commons that public concern for personal privacy ran 'very high', and with it was 'strong support for the kind of rights and safeguards introduced by data protection legislation' (House of Commons 1990, Minutes of evidence, p.1).

A questionnaire survey of 253 solicitors by Raymond Wacks in the early 1980s (before the Data Protection Act 1984) revealed a higher proportion than expected of people seeking legal advice about perceived 'problems' of privacy, including information privacy. Law centres had an even higher number of complaints. As Wacks points out, the high numbers may have been due to public expectations that there *should* be legal redress for these problems, regardless of whether there was. The survey also found that most solicitors felt there was no need for any change in the law (Wacks 1989, Chapter 4).

If information privacy is an easier target to focus on than privacy itself, we have only to consider ways in which the law can help 'police' the circulation of personal information with or without the consent of the person concerned. Laws and policies would give a degree of control back to that person to whom the information relates.

Personal information

If information privacy is our target, we must still define 'personal information'. Again there is no certainty as to what we mean by this term. In general terms, we might expect it to mean information relating to our family life, personal relationships and that which we consider private. It would include health and sexual matters, and anything which has no direct significance for the community at large. In short, it is anything we choose to call 'private and personal'. Wacks has proposed the following definition:

'Personal Information' consists of those facts, communications, or opinions which relate to the individual and which it would be reasonable to expect him (or her) to regard as intimate or sensitive and therefore to want to withhold or at least to restrict their collection, use, or circulation. (Wacks 1989, p. 26)

The Calcutt Committee inquiry into privacy came up with the following definition:

Personal information could be defined in terms of an individual's personal life, that is to say, those aspects of life which reasonable members of society would respect as being such that an individual is ordinarily entitled to keep them to himself, whether or not they relate to his mind or body, to his home, to other personal relationships, or to his correspondence or documents. (Home Office 1990a, para. 122.17)

What becomes eminently clear is that, however we define it, personal information is the very life-blood of work in the personal social services and is processed daily on a massive scale, whether as spoken word, written record, video cassette or computer record.

The Data Protection Act 1984 was circumspect in its definition, stating that personal information is only that which can be 'personally identified' (Section 1(3)). It did, however, recognise that some personal information was more sensitive than other personal information, and listed details of racial category, political or religious views, physical or mental health, sexual orientation and criminal conviction records as being such extra-sensitive information (Section 2(3)). These categories of sensitive personal information in the Data Protection Act are taken from the 1980 Council of Europe Convention on which the Act is based (Article 6). Other countries added to the list, and Denmark, for example, included colour of skin as sensitive information (see Stallworthy 1990). A private member's bill published July 1994 by MP Harry Cohen, suggested adding trade union membership and philosophical or ethical persuasions to the list, in keeping with the content of the European Union draft Directive on Data Protection (see also House of Lords 1993, paras 72–80).

The idea behind identifying these 'sensitive' categories was to enable extra safeguards to be built in to protect them against unauthorised disclosure. At present, no such extra safeguards have been devised in the UK, and this has upset some observers, who see these safeguards as the crux of good data protection legislation (Wacks 1989, p. 180). The Secretary of State appears to have no immediate plans to use powers under the Data Protection Act 1984 to produce regulations covering sensitive information (*Hansard*, 27 January 1994, PQ 210 WA).

It might be argued that personal information is not intrinsically sensitive in itself but is more dependent on the context in which it is placed. A person's address is sensitive information if someone is threatening to come around and smash their windows, but is not sensitive if they want a parcel sent to them. The address remains the same throughout, and only the context changes. Others disagree, and say that, whatever the context, personal information can and should be ranked in terms of sensitivity. Wacks has proposed a sensitivity index, based on reasonable assumptions of what is high, moderate and low-sensitivity personal information (Wacks 1989, pp. 222–38).

The UK law recognises the 'changing context' argument with respect to criminal convictions, for example. An adult appearing in court does so in the full glare of the public eye. His or her conviction and sentence can be given maximum publicity, dependent on the degree of public curiosity. It could be the front-page story in national newspapers or the lead item on the television news, or achieve just a small paragraph in the local paper.

After the court hearing, that same piece of personal information – the person's name, their conviction and sentence – experiences a change of context. It moves into a repository of personal information in a criminal record office, and a veil of confidentiality begins to fall around it. In due course, after a given period of time and if certain criteria are met, the record may be legally 'forgotten'. The Rehabilitation of Offenders Act 1974 accepts that some records may become 'spent' and do not have to be referred to again – indeed, to make an unauthorised disclosure may be a criminal offence (Section 9(2)). The same piece of 'neutral' personal information has moved from the public domain to the private without changing in content in any way.

Whether personal information is intrinsically sensitive or is made sensitive by its context, there is a degree to which people will claim 'ownership' of that information.

Ownership of personal information

The 'policing' of the circulation of personal information is usually only problematic when that circulation is without the consent of the person to whom the information applies. The idea of consent in turn leads to the belief that perhaps a person actually 'owns' that personal information, which is 'their' property to be controlled by them and disclosed only to people they choose. The question is then asked: 'Whose file is it anyway?' (Cohen 1982). In social work circles, it has been suggested that '"confidentiality" could be described ... as having to do with people's rights over the "property" of their secrets', and extracting those secrets under false pretences is a violation of personal rights akin to stealing (Butrym 1976, p. 51).

Claims to ownership of personal information are not that straightforward. Verbal information passed from one person to another is self-evidently not 'property' in any reasonable sense of the word. A manual file containing records of personal information might more properly belong to the agency holding it rather than the person it relates to. Personal information cannot be compared to 'intellectual property' such as a book, piece of music or an invention which can be protected by copyright or patent. Personal information may not even have been 'produced' by the person concerned. Consider the case of the person diagnosed HIV-positive, when it is the doctor rather than the person concerned who produces the information. The doctor could equally claim ownership.

In the USA, some consumer groups have organised themselves to try to charge commercial organisations using 'their' personal information. On receipt of computerised 'junk-mail' selling them various commodities, Citizens Inc. have turned the tables on the companies concerned by billing them for processing personal information held on them (Lyon 1994, p. 188). In precisely direct opposition to this, some workers in social services see case records as *their* property rather than the department's, let alone the client's. This is to take the *aide-mémoire* idea of records to its ultimate conclusion:

> My casework recordings have been made to help me and my professional colleagues to reach sensible casework decisions. If anyone else claims access to them, whether client or councillor, big brother or anyone else, I shall be taking steps to destroy those records as I would a personal diary similarly threatened with intrusion. (letter to *Community Care*, 26 August 1982)

To talk of the 'ownership' of personal information helps clarify some issues, such as consent, but it has its limitations when we start to explore it in more detail.

Conclusions

Having completed our brief history of privacy in Western liberal societies and started to look at some of the concepts we will be talking about, the intent for the remainder of the book is to locate those concepts in the context of social services work.

In Chapter 2 we consider the nature of privacy and the way in which social workers need to respect and uphold it, and what rights they have to 'breach' it. Chapter 3 looks at the various forms in which personal information is maintained in social services agencies, and Chapter 4 considers how the circulation of that information is regulated in the interests of information privacy. Chapter 5 explores the opening up of manual files and computer-held records to the subjects of those files and records, and Chapter 6 returns to the idea of privacy in the face of press and media reporting of personal social services 'stories'. Chapter 7 considers practical considerations governing the exchange of information between social workers and other agencies, and Chapter 8 surveys a number of developments in information technology and their implications for privacy.

2 Privacy and social services

If individuals, families and households are entitled to privacy, how do they maintain this privacy in the face of social services providers? If vulnerable people require care in the form of substitute homes, how do we respect their privacy when providing that care?

The ethos of social services work has always respected the integrity of individuals, families and other private households, and social workers sought to 'respect their clients as individuals and ... to ensure that their dignity, individuality, rights and responsibility shall be safeguarded' (BASW 1986). It is also true to say that social work and social services provision requires staff to enter the most private areas of life, and in social work 'privacy intrusion is just a fact of life' (Borkowski et al. 1983, p. 101). Such work is not by nature an intrusion if the people and families concerned have invited social services personnel in. Most work does indeed fall into this category when requests are made for community care provisions, aids to disability or problems with child care. Some interventions are equally clearly not welcomed by the recipients and are considered intrusive.

Social services practitioners have sought to justify their intrusions on people's privacy by reference to themselves as representatives of the 'public interest', or alternatively, as acting in the 'best interests' of the person intruded upon. They have, for example, argued that, in the field of child protection, they sometimes have to make decisions to override the rights to privacy of the adults concerned in the interests of a child's right to live an abuse-free life.

Throughout the 1970s, these feelings were further brought home by the rise of the women's movement, and later the children's rights movement. Within the confines of the home, both women and children were suffering a range of abuses at the hands of men, and for them the concept of 'privacy' in terms of the home meant very little. Agencies such as the police and social workers were called on to intervene more positively (see also Parton 1991, pp. 196–7). The very terminology – domestic violence – was rounded on as being too cosy and diverting attention away from what was really criminal violence within the home (Maguire 1988).

All such rationales for intrusion can be subsumed into acting in the 'public interest' and, as such, are given public sanction in various statutes. At its most extreme are the warrants issued by magistrates that allow social services staff to enter premises with the police, using force if necessary, in order to carry out their task. Such intrusions of privacy are particular to certain circumstances, which need to be expressed to the magistrate in advance. Other more general rights of entry exist if courts have made orders of varying terms in length – usually in terms of supervision in the 'public interest' – that a social worker has an obligation to carry through.

Local authority social workers have no statutory rights of entry by virtue of their status alone, and only the common law would protect them from civil actions, where they would need to argue, for example, that they were acting to save life and limb. In all other situations, social workers and other social services staff must rely on an invitation to enter a household, unless they are enacting a specific statute.

At its most simple level, the provision of social services to people in their own homes is made either with or without consent. If a person requests a service and gives consent to entering their premises, it is usually an unproblematic business. Consent, however, is not always a straightforward matter. In practice, it can take on an air of unreality when people are not aware of their rights and feel that anyone 'official', like a social worker, has an automatic right to come into their house or flat. In turn, social workers can play on this ignorance and not even ask the direct question as to whether they can come in. (We return to some of the complexities of consent in Chapter 4.)

Consent can also be withdrawn at any time, and social workers who enter premises with the consent of the occupier but are then asked to leave have no alternative but to leave unless they have a warrant or a statutory right to be there. Failure to leave after being requested to do so would render the social worker a trespasser, and the occupier would be entitled to use 'reasonable force' to remove him or her.

If a person has not consented, and others feel the service must be imposed in the interests, perhaps, of a vulnerable individual such as a child within a given household, then the invasion of privacy is more clear-cut. Such compulsory intervention, without consent and with access to given premises probably refused, is the exception rather than the rule, but at times has to be carried through. Where is the right to privacy in these circumstances? A priority for all social services workers in such situations is to be able to identify themselves and know the legal authority that is empowering them to act.

Identification

In the 'city of strangers' we need to be able to identify ourselves. We live in a 'credentialist' society, and all social services employees visiting people at home need to be able to identify themselves. Local authority social workers investigating child protection issues are expected to 'produce some duly authenticated document' if called upon, to prove who they are (Children Act 1989, Section 44(3)). A similar document is necessary in carrying out formal inspections of childminding arrangements and private day nurseries (Section 76(6)) and of private fostering arrangements (Section 67(4)). Local authority employees charged with inspecting voluntary children's homes and independent schools should also be able to produce identification (Sections 62(7) and 87(7)). In practice, one composite ID card would be given to a worker.

A social worker who has become an 'approved social worker' within the meaning of the Mental Health Act 1983 must also produce identification in carrying out duties under that Act. The production of a 'duly authenticated document' allows the approved social worker to enter and inspect any premises, at any reasonable time, other than a hospital, to see a mentally disordered person if it is believed the patient is not under proper care (Mental Health Act 1983, Section 115). It does not allow forced entry to premises, although refusal to permit entry would constitute an offence under Section 129 of the Mental Health Act.

Private residential care homes for mentally disordered people, or indeed for children or elderly people, may be entered by authorised social services staff using the Registered Homes Act 1984, Section 17(1). Again it is an offence to obstruct someone so authorised from entering (Section 17(b)), and again 'some duly authenticated document' showing authority to exercise this power must be produced if asked for (Section 17(5)). Similar powers exist for the inspection of mental nursing homes, although the inspector might be a member of health services rather than social services staff (Section 35).

In most cases a householder will not ask to see a social worker's identification card, but it would be good practice always to show it, whether or not it has been asked for. In these circumstances, access to a house is usually offered and not contested by the person concerned. The first half of 1990 saw the rise of an epidemic of 'bogus social workers' in the UK that spread rapidly across the country. The police received reports of people claiming to be social workers, making home visits and asking to examine children. The media jumped on the bandwagon, and theories were thrown around, as to what these imposters were trying to achieve (see, for example, Oulton 1990). The BASW called on all local authorities to ensure that identity cards were adequate, and carried a photograph and a telephone number to verify the bearer's identity (Neate 1990). As mysteriously as this 'epidemic' had begun, so it ended. A meeting in June 1990 of 23 police forces who had investigated the phenomenon revealed that, of 173 sightings of bogus social workers, all but 18 could be innocently explained and were in no way sinister ('Bogus visits not UK-linked', *Community Care*, 7 June 1990). The media lost interest, and the whole show collapsed. Nothing more was heard of the 'epidemic', although odd reports still come in from time to time (see, for example, 'Bogus Workers', *Community Care*, 31 March 1994).

It has been suggested that all UK citizens carry an ID card, and not just social workers. From 1939 to 1952, all citizens did carry an ID card as part of the Wartime National Registration Scheme. The scheme was dropped after a Liberal parliamentary candidate, Harry Willcock, decided to make a stand and refused to produce the card on demand to a police officer as he was statutorily required to do. Willcock was convicted but received an absolute discharge, and after further parliamentary discussion, the government decided to repeal the National Registration Act 1939 which had introduced ID cards (*Willcock v. Muckle* [1952] 1 KB 367; see also Dovey 1986).

In 1985 the police put forward the idea that mentally impaired people should carry an ID card so that the police would be aware if they arrested someone with limited intelligence. The idea was suggested in the context of the closure of long-term hospitals in favour of care in the community policies (House of Commons 1985, para. 139). A few years later an attempt was made to get all football supporters to carry an ID card to help with the policing of football matches, but following Lord Justice Taylor's final report on the Hillsborough Stadium disaster, the government decided against implementing the relevant sections of the Football Spectators Act 1989. More recently, the police have again suggested ID cards as a way of fighting crime, and not least in the context of going into Europe, where frontiers were being opened and a freer movement of people was anticipated within the European Union. The ID card was seen as a 'compensatory measure' for the lowering of border controls and the perceived loss of so-called 'squeeze points' at customs and immigration offices on the UK borders (Lyon 1991).

Of more direct relevance to social service workers was the suggestion that social security claimants should carry ID cards to cut down the amount of fraud taking place. The idea was first floated by the right-wing No Turning Back Group (1993) and then taken up by government ministers ('Civil Liberties concern at threat of social security ID cards', *The Independent*, 25 October 1993). The Secretary of State, Peter Lilley, proposed that people be asked to give palmprints before claiming their state pensions ('Lilley floats palmprints scheme', *The Independent*, 26 October 1993).

Whilst these ideas for a piecemeal introduction of ID cards continue to circulate, the arguments about the national ID card remain rumbling in the background. The civil liberties arguments have been put, and the need for large database facilities against which to match cards has been considered, along with the need to give police (and possibly social workers) new powers to enforce production of a card (see, for example, NCCL 1988). At governmental level, views varied from Prime Minister John Major's belief that ID cards would help combat crime (Jones, G. 1994) to Lord Ferers' statement that, even as a means of tackling terrorism, 'I.D. cards do not feature high on the list' (*Hansard*, HL Deb., Vol. 545, Col. 1 650, 18 May 1993). It was in this context that the Data Protection Registrar called for a full public debate on the need for ID cards, because: 'the issue is too fundamental for the UK to allow itself to slip into having a de facto national identification system' (DPR 1994, p. 10), and in October 1994 the Home Secretary announced his intention to put out a consultation paper on the subject ('ID cards come a step nearer', *The Independent*, 14 October 1994).

Denial of access

Although there is no law defining privacy, we have already noted that the laws of trespass enable a person to ask people to leave their premises and permit use of 'reasonable force' to eject them. It is possible to lead a life reasonably free from intrusion; on the other hand, it still comes as a shock to us when people who lived close by lie dead behind their closed doors for lengthy periods. When a 69-year-old man was found in London four years after his death, the coroner proclaimed: 'this is the most extraordinary case that has come to the notice of any court I've been involved in' ('Council tenant lay dead in flat for four years', *The Independent*, 18 March 1994).

A social worker's failure to gain access to premises is a 'problem' given the context in which the call is made. Social workers are amongst a number of 'official' figures who have the authority – or can apply for authority – to enter a person's home without their consent. Normally, such an entrance would constitute trespass. As we have seen, there is no general law protecting the privacy of a household, and each 'official' breach of that privacy is defined in statutes or common law (for a brief survey of all official rights of entry see 'A foot in the door', *Which?*, September 1993, pp. 38–41; for a definitive legal overview see Stone 1989). Often the failure to gain access is a cumulative problem. In child protection work, one health visitor called 23 times but only gained access to a house on 9 occasions. The child eventually died, and the resulting inquiry report recommended better training on the significance of 'no access visits' (Leicestershire County Council 1980).

If access cannot be obtained, then the purpose of the social worker's visit should dictate the action that needs to follow. A conversation through a window may be sufficient in some cases but not others. The Department of Health has specifically stated that approved social workers acting within the meaning of the Mental Health Act 1983 must carry out assessments by interviewing people in a 'suitable manner' (Section 13(2)), and this in turn means:

> It is not desirable for a patient to be interviewed through a closed door or window except where there is serious risk to other people. Where there is no immediate risk of physical danger to the patient or to others, powers in the Act to secure access [section 135] should be used. (DoH 1993a, para. 2.11(f))

The Report of the Inquiry into the death of Kimberley Carlile was also clear that the social worker being permitted by a hostile adult 'to peep through the small glass panel at the top of the door to one of the children's bedrooms' was not a sufficient form of assessment given the concerns about the child's welfare. In this instance the social worker had gained access to the premises but not to the actual child, who remained effectively an 'unseen' child (London Borough of Greenwich 1987, p. 115).

It is perhaps also worth noting at this point that the courts have ruled that the owner or co-owner of premises is entitled to allow entry to another person, including a police officer or social worker, even if the owner or co-owner is not the person being sought (*Slade* v. *Guscott* (28 July 1981) CA 78/ 06556 (unreported), cited in Gostin 1986, para. 21.13.5). A local authority has a duty to investigate any possible child abuse in its area if information is brought to its attention. Social workers seeking access to children to assure themselves of the child's exact circumstances may seek powers under the Children Act to help them carry out their investigation.

It is equally true to say that most child protection investigations of this kind do not require additional powers, and members of the public usually assist without recourse to magistrates' orders. If powers are required at short notice, the central provision is that of the Emergency Protection Order (EPO) available under the Children Act 1989, Section 44, to which various ancilliary powers can be added. The EPO enables the holder to remove a child from a household if he or she is thought likely to suffer significant harm, or to detain a child by preventing others from removing him or her from a 'safe' place, such as a hospital.

In applying to a magistrate for an EPO, the applicant can request certain 'additions'. The Department of Health suggests that some of these 'additions' should be routinely applied for to enhance the basic EPO. The Children Act 1989, Section 48(1), empowers the social worker to demand information on the whereabouts of the child if he or she cannot immediately be found; failure to provide this information puts a person in contempt of court. Section 48(3) of the Children Act authorises the social worker with the EPO to enter and search premises; failure to allow access is a criminal offence (DoH 1991a, paras 4.50 and 4.52). The ultimate sanction of the investigating social worker is to apply for the EPO to be given additional powers of entry using reasonable force if necessary. The magistrate will issue a warrant naming a constable to enter the premises, either with or without the social worker, to seek access to the child in question. The magistrate will not add this power as a routine matter, but only when he or she is satisfied that the applicant has tried to gain access and been refused, and is likely to be so again (Children Act 1989, Section 48(9) and 48(10)).

Under the old law, two high-profile child abuse inquiry reports had taken issue with the earlier legal provisions of the Children and Young Persons Act 1933, Section 40. In the London Borough of Hillingdon, police had used a warrant to break in and search for Lisa Koseda, a named child on the warrant, in December 1984. Once Lisa was found well and healthy the terms of the warrant were terminated, and there was no general requirement to check on other children. The other children would have included 4-year-old Heidi Koseda, Lisa's sister, whose body was found on 23 January 1985 in a state of starvation. In this case the report called for changes in the law to widen the powers of Section 40 (London Borough of Hillingdon Area Review Committee 1986). The report of the inquiry into the death of Kimberley Carlile, aged 4 years, was more perturbed because of the seeming ignorance of social workers regarding the very existence of Section 40 of the Children and Young Persons Act 1933. Whilst recognising the 'fine balance' needed between unnecessary interference in family life and the need to protect children (London Borough of Greenwich 1987, p. 144) the report found: 'Social workers ... reluctant to use this power – even if they have been aware of its existence, which many have not – except when they are absolutely certain that such a step is necessary' (p. 149).

Criticisms have also been made of the timing of these forced 'child protection' entries to houses. Of particular notoriety have been the so-called 'dawn raids' on houses, which gave the impression of an inordinate degree of force being used in these combined police–social work operations. The raids could be construed as traumatic to children and parents alike, and with the possibility of long-term damage to family relationships. Reports suggested that 'dawn raids' continued to be used (see 'Fury over dawn raid', *Social Work Today*, 13 September 1990), and in 1992 attention was further drawn to the ruling of Justice Hollings in the Family Division, that:

> early morning removals of children from their home, by police, even though in conjunction with social services, should only be effected when there are clear grounds for believing significant harm would otherwise be caused to the chil-

dren or vital evidence is only obtainable by such means. (*Re A and Others (Minors)* [1992] 1 FLR 439)

The Department of Health specifically advises against the early-morning raid, unless it is unavoidable. It is suggested that it is really only necessary when, say, a number of adults are suspected of the abuse of children, and they need to be arrested and prevented from communicating with each other (Home Office et al. 1991, para. 3.8). Similar provisions exist to force entry to recover children who have run away from care or are simply missing but believed to be in hiding at certain addresses. Again the order – a Recovery Order – is made out to a constable, who may use reasonable force if necessary to enter the premises. Comparable powers also exist to permit entry and to require people to give information on the whereabouts of children (Children Act 1989, Section 50).

Approved social workers within the meaning of the Mental Health Act 1983 are permitted access to inspect premises, visit or examine mentally disordered people and look at records kept on mentally disordered residents. As we have seen, anyone who obstructs an officer carrying out these duties without 'reasonable cause' is guilty of an offence. The point has also been made that approved social workers entering premises with a view to applying for hospital admission under Part II of the Mental Health Act 1983 are required to interview people 'in a suitable manner' (Section 13(2)). The Code of Practice accompanying the Act elaborates on what 'in a suitable manner' means, and although it suggests that, where possible, the approved social worker should see the patient alone (DoH 1993a, para. 2.12), there is nothing comparable to the statutory requirement in the Act for a doctor to see the patient in 'private' (Mental Health Act 1983, Section 24(1); see Jones, R. 1994, paras 1–138).

A forced entry to a house may be made if it is believed that someone inside is suffering from a mental disorder and is living alone and unable to care for themselves, or is living with someone but being ill-treated or neglected (see also Pidgeon and Bates 1990). An approved social worker must apply to a magistrate for an order permitting such a break-in, and the order is executed by a police officer named in the warrant. It is necessary to name the premises concerned, but not necessarily the person if he or she is not known. If it is 'thought fit', the person can be compulsorily removed and held for 72 hours. The law is not explicit as to who makes the decision to remove after entry has been made, but it would seem that the approved social worker and the registered medical practitioner who must accompany the police officer, rather than the police officer, should make the decision (Mental Health Act 1983, Sections 135(1) and 135(3–4)).

A patient liable to detention who has left a hospital and is refusing to allow people into an address to take him or her back can also be subject to

an application to a magistrate for an order allowing forced entry and removal. Any social worker can make this application, and it need not be an
approved social worker. The premises and person concerned must be named
in the application, and the named police officer executing the warrant may
be accompanied by a doctor and social worker. The police could execute the
warrant alone if they wished (Mental Health Act 1983, Sections 135(2) and
135(3–4)).

A police officer has the right to enter premises without a warrant in an
emergency where 'life and limb' may be at risk (Police and Criminal Evidence Act 1984, Section 17(1)(e)) and also the right to enter premises if
actively pursuing a person he or she knows is unlawfully at large and liable
to detention somewhere (Section 17(1)(d)). In the first instance, this might
include women and children who are at risk of violence within the home. In
the second instance, the critical word is 'actively' pursuing, because the
Law Lords have ruled it unlawful to use this power simply to enter premises
where a person is believed to be (*D'Souza* v. *DPP* [1992] 4 All ER HL 546).

The police have powers to act alone to remove people from a public place
who appear to be mentally distressed and in need of care, and to do so
compulsorily if necessary. It is worth noting that a public place is defined as
'a place to which the public have access' (Mental Health Act 1983, Section
136). This is taken to mean public houses, shops, theatres or sports grounds
that are otherwise private premises. A communal balcony in a block of flats
also counts as a public place (*Carter* v. *Metropolitan Police Commissioner*
[1975] 1 WLR 507), but once inside a flat or household, Section 136 is no
longer available to the police officer (see also *McConnell* v. *Chief Constable of
Greater Manchester Police* [1990] 1 All ER 423 CA for a further debate on
private–public space and law relating to breach of the peace).

The police have additional powers to apply to a magistrate for a warrant
to forcibly enter premises where a woman may be being detained for purposes of unlawful sexual intercourse; the Act specifically mentions women
who are mentally impaired as being in need of these protective provisions
(Sexual Offences Act 1956, Section 43).

The circumstances surrounding the death of 23-year-old Beverley Lewis,
in her own home, in February 1989 caused renewed debate on social work
powers of forced intervention. Beverley was mentally impaired, deaf and
blind and received constant care from her mother. When she died she
weighed only 4 stones, and the cause of death was recorded as emaciation
and pneumonia (Johnson 1989). The lack of care given to Beverley was
attributed to her mother's own mental ill-health. Mrs Thelma Lewis was
assessed as living with schizophrenia, and it was the presence of a second
person in the home, rather than Beverley simply living alone, that caused
difficulties for the professionals involved. Beverley had been compulsorily
removed on one occasion (under the Mental Health Act 1983, Section 135),

only to be returned because her mother agreed to visits from a community psychiatric nurse. Guardianship (Mental Health Act 1983, Sections 7–10) had also been ruled out as a possibility (see also Fennel 1989).

The National Assistance Act 1948 was also considered as a way of intervening in the home life of Beverley Lewis and her mother. The Act allows the compulsory removal of people who are suffering from serious illness, living in insanitary conditions and receiving insufficient care (National Assistance Act 1948, Section 47). Some 200 people – usually elderly people – are compulsorily removed by this Act every year, even though mental disorder does not have to be present (Age Concern 1986, Chapter 2). The Act does *not* give powers to force entry, and although the degree of illness and incapacity present would probably result in little resistance, the question of 'real' consent to enter could be problematic.

Powers to force entry do exist in these circumstances, to ascertain whether there are or have been any contraventions of the Public Health Act 1936, Section 287(1), but the powers would be applied by local authority environmental health officers rather than social services staff. A local authority also has powers to require a person to leave property that needs fumigating, and has a duty to offer them alternative accommodation until the property is safe to reoccupy (Public Health Act 1961, Section 36).

Section 47 of the National Assistance Act has been the subject of rumbling criticism for a number of years. Denounced as an 'anachronism' and as a 'cloak for inadequate social services' (Tregaskis and Mayberry 1994), the suggestion is that we would not need it if we had decent community care services. The Law Commission has recommended the repeal of Section 47 and its replacement with a new power for social workers to enter premises where it is believed an incapacitated, mentally disordered or vulnerable person is living and is suspected of suffering or being likely to suffer significant harm; a power to force entry with the police would be added if needed (Law Commission 1993, paras 3.25 and 3.30); the British Association of Social Workers has suggested similar powers when local authority social workers need immediate access to protect a disabled adult (BASW 1990, p. 5).

Organising fieldwork services

A continuing debate on the provision of social services in a given community concerns the way in which that provision is organised. Methods exist on a continuum between centralised and decentralised services – from the ideal of the bureaucratic, remote and centralised office through to the more flexible, relevant, local 'patch' team close to the community it serves. The way in which fieldwork services are organised can have a bearing on the intrusiveness – or otherwise – of social services as experienced by the community.

The idea of decentralised services close to the people they serve was contained in the Seebohm Report, which gave birth to today's social services departments: 'The staff of the social services department will need to see themselves not as a self-contained unit but as part of a network of services within the community' (Seebohm Report 1968, para. 478). The reality did not match these early ideals as, throughout the 1970s, social services departments grew into large bureaucracies modelled on other traditional local authority departments, and sometimes referred to as 'Seebohm factories'. Only later came the re-evaluation that perhaps a decentralised service might be more relevant, and in particular the re-evaluation by the Barclay Report in 1982. The Barclay Report generally favoured the decentralised or community social work approach. The report also contained within it the opposing arguments to decentralisation in a dissenting Appendix B, which, amongst other things, raised the question of privacy in relation to social services provision. Being pro-active in providing preventive social services was all very well, but preventive social work was also 'an insidious threat to privacy because it can always be "justified" on grounds of social welfare'. In fact, apart from being a local constant presence, there would be an 'indiscriminate collection of information' which could be 'potentially lethal to our civil liberties' (Barclay Report 1982, p. 255).

In the event, the financial constraints on local government have effectively stopped any models of community social work developing in anything like the social controlling form described in Appendix B. Social services departments, whether decentralised or not, do accumulate and store a great deal of personal information, as we shall consider later, but any constant presence seems hardly to have materialised.

For their part, communities have not always been willing to play their part in community-based 'patch' services. On one level, what is so wonderful about being told there are no resources available for you by an office round the corner compared to one further away? On another, there is the ever-present suspicion of some communities regarding the presence of 'the welfare' or any other representative of 'authority' encamped on their doorsteps. Part of the rationale of decentralised services is to pick up information early and to co-ordinate with other local agencies to prevent situations deteriorating. If the information is not forthcoming, there is a natural restraint on any preventive work.

One concerted attempt to organise communities into 'information-producing systems' has been the instigation of Neighbourhood Watch projects, whereby residents co-ordinate their 'watching' activities to try to reduce levels of crime. The police often take the lead in getting schemes off the ground, and in some areas, such as Cambridgeshire, have even entered into arrangements to have designated electronic mail links between the police force and watch co-ordinators. Overall, however, research suggests Neighbourhood Watch has a limited impact, and apathy amongst participants is always likely to set in (Bennett 1990).

Of more direct concern to social services might be the schemes modelled on Neighbourhood Watch, such as Childwatch or Truancy Watch, to encourage the reporting of children who look as though they should be at school. Truancy Watch schemes are said to have originated in the Staffordshire area, where the police and education welfare officers co-opted the help of shopkeepers and others in the community – usually a town centre – to send in information on suspected truants in an area: 'A truant will, if possible, have their name, address, school and a brief physical description placed on to a confidential referral form and this will be forwarded to Education Welfare' (Staffordshire Police 1993).

This exercise could be seen as an invasion of privacy or a genuine attempt to re-create the simple society of old, where everyone watched everyone else. The then Secretary of State for Education certainly liked the idea, and adjusted grants for education support and training to encourage the setting up of Truancy Watch schemes (see, for example, 'Adults must report truants, Patten says', *The Independent*, 27 November 1993).

Providing residential care

Local authority personal social services provide a range of residential care facilities for children and adults who cannot be looked after in any other way. Local authorities also work closely with similar facilities in the voluntary and private sector, where they have additional responsibilities to regulate provisions.

It has long been held that residents of any age in residential care have a right to a degree of privacy in these communal living arrangements. Indeed, it has been suggested that people living in care 'need more privacy than in a family because of the greater likelihood of encroachments' (Clough 1982, p. 60).

Children and young persons

The physical space and layout of a children's home must now allow for showers, toilets and bathing areas to be private areas (DoH 1991b, para. 1.69) and ensure elsewhere the necessary:

opportunities for complete privacy. The design of the home must recognise the need for both companionship and privacy. A flexible approach is needed to take into account the children's wishes to make sure that personal items of furniture, personal pictures, possessions, ornaments or models can be kept to enhance and personalise that child's surroundings. (para. 1.62)

The Children's Homes Regulations (SI 1991 No. 1506) reinforce this guidance by making it mandatory to provide facilities for private meetings with parents, solicitors, guardians ad litem, relatives, friends and others (Regulation 7(3)) and to ensure that all children have access to a pay phone where they can make private phone calls (Regulation 7(5)).

Privacy for parents visiting for contact with children is further encouraged by Department of Health guidance that, whether in children's homes or foster-care, 'privacy and a welcoming and congenial setting are available' for contact (DoH 1991b, para. 4.18). It is recognised that sometimes, in the interests of child protection, contact with parents and others may have to be supervised (para. 4.26), and that in such cases privacy will be intruded upon by the presence of a member of the social services department's staff.

Residential social services staff have to use their professional skills to ensure an element of privacy exists for children and young people on an everyday basis. Good relationships in the home are the bedrock of a stable environment for residents, and at times this will need the support of various sanctions to ensure an ordered way of life in the home. In balancing these positive and negative elements of residential child care, staff have to avoid the worst excesses of control, such as the 'Pindown' scandal of the Staffordshire children's homes (Levy and Kahan 1991). At a more prosaic level, children have complained:

> The trouble with care is there is no place to sulk. If you are upset, perhaps something has gone wrong at home, or for whatever reason, there's no place to have a sulk, the staff pop up wherever you go. (Page and Clark 1977, p. 26)

Enhanced supervision of children in homes has been promoted more generally as a way of controlling disruptive children. In response to a perceived public concern, the Department of Health has published suggestions on how disruptive children could better be physically restrained and be subject to what it called 'permissible' forms of control, (DoH 1993b). Closer supervision might prevent absconding as well as misbehaviour, and 'at its simplest level a staff member's presence in the room with children should be a deterrent to misbehaviour' (para. 10.2). Younger children might also be watched when they go into unsafe areas either inside or outside the home (para. 8.4). Closer supervision inevitably means less privacy.

The Department of Health is conscious that it is walking a fine line between acceptable controls and unacceptable forms of control that veer into abusive regimes. Children may be taken out of the group 'into a calming environment' (para. 8.3) but should never be subject to the isolation regimes and deprivation of the 'Pindown' experiments in Staffordshire (Levy and Kahan 1991). The holding and touching of children is permissible to enable staff to express 'parental' affection towards children, but age and gender should be taken into account, and 'there should be no general expectations of privacy for the physical expression of affection or comfort' (DoH 1993b, para. 10.6). The Department of Health stays on the right side of acceptability, but openly accepts that earlier advice 'may have gone too far in stressing the rights of children at the expense of upholding the rights and responsibilities of parents and professionals in supervising them' (para. 1.1).

What we are seeing here are the dilemmas of balancing collective living for often damaged children with the need to encourage individuality with appropriate amounts of privacy. The balance is not an easy one, and is always made in a wider public context that lacks sympathy for many young people who find themselves looked after by local authorities (often assumed to all be criminals) and is easily persuaded that young people's rights do not necessarily have a priority.

Telephones in children's homes are seen as an important way of allowing children to keep in touch with their families and the outside world. The idea was given a boost by the introduction of Childline in October 1986. Childline was a telephone help-line enabling troubled children to talk to qualified social workers and counsellors. Described as a 'children's Samaritans', the scheme was launched by television personality Esther Rantzen's *Child Watch* programme and gave young people a freephone number to call in ('Free phone for abused children', *Social Work Today*, 13 October 1986, p. 4).

The Children Act 1989 brought in regulations requiring all children's homes to have a pay telephone installed where children could make and receive calls in private (Children's Homes Regulations 1991, Regulation 7(5)). A later Department of Health survey on telephone provision had to admit a 'surprisingly disappointing response', with less than half the authorities concerned having 'complied fully or largely with this requirement' (Department of Health 1993c, para. 5.24). The DoH was forced to speculate that 'what is worrying is the possibility that this failure to install telephones may indicate a custodial attitude towards children in residential care' (para. 5.24); the shortfall was still there in 1994 (SSI 1994a, p. 22).

Critical to the provision of the telephones was the requirement that they be in a private area of the home. In the past, staff had been known to eavesdrop on conversations or even deliberately tape telephone conversations (Chamberlain 1987). Such activities are surely against the welfare of the child, and have been recognised as such. The Children's Legal Centre tried unsuccessfully to get an amendment added to the Interception of Communications Act 1985 to protect children in care ('Letters and 'phone calls in care – privacy rights sought in new Bill', *Childright*, No. 17, May 1985).

Privacy is also to be created for children in order to help them pursue their religious observance. The Children Act 1989 was seen as setting new standards by placing a general duty on all local authorities looking after children to give due consideration to 'the child's religious persuasion, racial origin and cultural and linguistic background' (Section 22(5)(c)). In turn, this might mean allowing a child 'special privacy in order to pray during the course of the day' (Department of Health 1991b, para. 1.124).

Officers in charge or managers of residential units for children, or indeed for adults, may find themselves in the position of defending the privacy of residents against outside requests from the police to search their unit. We might surmise that such searches would be to look for, say, stolen property, illegal drugs or offensive weapons, and that the police making the request were seeking consent to a search. Residential staff would need to decide if the resident should have a say in consenting to the search, and whether the search should be limited to part of the residential unit or be more widespread (see Thomas 1994a, pp. 104–5).

The police could demand entry with a warrant to search, which would make consent unnecessary. The warrant must have been signed by a magistrate and would need to be checked to see that it states the grounds for the application, specifies the appropriate premises and identifies as far as practicable the articles or persons to be sought (Police and Criminal Evidence Act 1984, Section 15).

Entry can also be demanded without a search warrant in order to search for a person who is subject to a warrant of arrest, a warrant of commitment under the Magistrates Court Act 1980, Section 76, to recapture an escapee, look for an offensive weapon, to save life or limb, or to arrest a person for an arrestable offence (Police and Criminal Evidence Act 1984, Section 17; see also Littlechild 1994, pp. 89–92).

The Home Office guidance to the police on searching premises that are occupied communally is not very clear when it comes to social services residential care, with merely a reference to 'the case of a lodging house or similar accommodation [when] a search should not be made on the basis solely of the landlord's consent unless the tenant is unavailable and the matter is urgent' (Home Office 1991a, Code B, para. 4A). We would need to consider that the words 'similar accommodation' covered social services residential care provision for the guidance to be applicable.

Allegations are still made that the privacy of children in residential care is breached, and secure accommodation units, for example, use closed-circuit television systems and two-way mirror screens to observe children, 'not necessarily with their knowledge let alone their agreement' (Newell 1991, p. 59). In one local authority, staff had received no guidance on privacy or confidentiality, and had freely entered children's bedrooms without knocking (SSI 1993a, pp. 20–1). Locks had been reported missing from bathroom and toilet doors, and unacceptable glass partitions had been put in bedroom doors (*ibid*). A wider study of residential child care services in 11 local authorities confirmed a dismal picture (SSI 1993b, paras 5.21–5.40).

Finally, in relation to children, we might note a new child protection technique called 'covert video surveillance' which has quietly come into being. At present it is only used in hospitals, rather than residential care where the aim would be to secretly record parental interaction with children in an effort to 'capture' on film deliberate attempts to injure the child (see also pages 51–52).

Adults

The government-sponsored code of practice for residential care, *Home Life*, was aimed at all user groups, but was essentially applicable to residential care homes for elderly people. The code argued for privacy and autonomy for all residents, meaning they should have their own rooms and be encouraged to personalise their private space with their own soft furnishings, ornaments, pictures and plants. Toilet facilities should be private even when a disability meant a person needed help, and residents should have access to a private telephone to make external calls (Centre for Policy on Ageing 1984, p. 23). Later guidance and recommendations repeated the argument that privacy was central to good residential care (Wagner Report 1988; DoH 1989a).

The Social Services Inspectorate also confirmed that 'privacy' was a fundamental belief that should underpin the provision of residential care for elderly people, and they had a 'right to be alone or undisturbed and free from intrusion, or public attention in relation to individuals and their affairs' (SSI 1990, p. 5). A 'good' home would ensure privacy by taking into account such factors as:

- the resident's previous lifestyle and expectations of privacy;
- residents' preferences;
- arrangements for residents to discuss personal matters with staff and visitors in private;
- ensuring staff deal discreetly with the affairs of residents and safeguard the confidentiality of information held about them;
- ensuring any necessary erosion of privacy to provide essential care is explained, justified and reviewed regularly (see SSI 1990, p. 29 for a complete list).

By way of underlining this fundamental right, the 'Citizen's Charter' launched by the Prime Minister's Office in July 1991 also contained a brief reference to the need for 'privacy, quality of life and respect for individuality in residential homes' (Citizen's Charter 1991, p. 21).

Any attempts to improve rights to privacy in residential care have to be balanced between physical and spatial dimensions of privacy and the more intangible aspects of staff attitudes and behaviour. As children's privacy might be curtailed in the interests of discipline and control, so adults might find their privacy intruded upon in the interest of protective care of those who are particularly vulnerable.

It is this need to protect the very vulnerable elderly or disabled person that is usually cited by residential staff who enter rooms without knocking, or do not allow locks to be put on bathroom or toilet doors. At worst, however, such attitudes demonstrate an infantilising of elderly people or disabled people by staff that often pride themselves on offering 'intimate, homely' atmospheres without realising the inappropriateness of adopting what becomes a 'parental' rather than a 'professional' role. The same attitudes contribute to the idea that the task of residential care is essentially an amateur one (see, for example, Counsel and Care 1991, p. 9).

Residential care homes bring together elderly people who are often complete strangers and bring with them no expectations of joining a 'family'. Many may have lived alone for a number of years and find the collective life of residential care extremely difficult to cope with. Differing individual needs for privacy will exist that should be met with an individual response and not a blanket regulatory approach applicable to everyone. Even the need for a single rather than a shared room and such basic requirements as a curtained-off commode have sometimes been found wanting. The research already cited found numerous examples of privacy being denied in residential care, and even worse, a low expectation on the part of residents that they should be able to expect privacy. They concluded that 'the attitude of the staff, particularly that of the head of the home, is the most critical factor in promoting and maintaining good standards of privacy' (Counsel and Care 1991, p. 4).

Attempts by some private residential care homes to install closed-circuit television cameras in the public areas of homes were met with vigorous opposition as an invasion of privacy. A proprietor of a home in Kirklees appealed to a registered homes tribunal, arguing that cameras were an aid to safety, especially for residents with dementia. The tribunal dismissed the appeal and stated its belief that 'the very existence of closed-circuit television in a residential care home is objectionable' ('TV Camera Ban in Homes', *Social Work Today*, 10 May 1990). Similar views were expressed when a home in Humberside experimented with electronic monitoring of residents thought likely to wander off. An electronic device was placed in a resident's shoe, and if it passed over an invisible sensor in the ground it set off a flashing alarm in the staff office ('Humberside launches six-month tagging experiment', *Social Work Today*, 16 February 1989).

These innovations in technology will always be controversial when attempts are made to implement them in welfare work. No matter how effective they may be, the underlying ethical base of social services work still seems strong enough to question them when human dignity is put at risk.

All residential care, for whatever age group, tries to be as non-institutional as possible and to 'normalise' home life for its residents. Care and control of people who are deviant or otherwise vulnerable has to be effective at the same time as recognising individual rights in a collective living environment.

In its wider sense, we are also now beginning to talk about the boundaries of professionalism and what does and does not constitute a breach of those boundaries. Social services workers – either in residential or fieldwork – can arguably allow their private life to intrude into that of the service users. Fieldworkers who work late into the evening or give out their home telephone numbers to clients run the risk of confusing their professional and private lives (see also BASW 1986, para. 10(vi)). At worst, this leads down the path to unacceptable relationships with clients, sexual relations and even sexual abuse of residents in care. At this point the recruitment and selection of staff as well as appropriate training and management all play their part to avoid the worst excesses of unprofessional behaviour (see, for example, Levy and Kahan 1991).

3 Personal information and social services

Having considered the nature of privacy in social services work, we now need to turn to information privacy. Earlier we noted that social services agencies are privy to large amounts of sensitive personal information. In this chapter we look at the forms in which that information is kept, and in Chapter 4 we consider the way in which its circulation is 'policed' both within social services agencies and between agencies, in what we might call the 'welfare network'.

The definitive history of record-keeping and personal information storage in the provision of personal social services has probably yet to be written. Enough sources exist, however, to piece together some of the developments which gave rise to today's social services agencies and the ways in which they maintain records of personal information.

A historical view

The Charity Organisation Society (COS) is generally considered to be the founder of modern social work with its attempts to organise the giving of charity. The COS also introduced the idea of the 'case-file' – or 'case-paper', as they preferred to call it – as an integral part of the work. As we saw in Chapter 1, if charity was to be given to 'strangers', then attempts had to be made to 'know' these strangers, and to know them in a formal way by recording information about them. On the basis of this written information, a decision could be made to give or withhold assistance and to attach conditions if necessary. The resulting case-paper put together by the COS has been described by one researcher as an 'awesome document': 'throughout, visits, interviews and action taken were recorded in the case-paper.

Letters to the committee and copies of letters from the office, and other relevant material, such as press cuttings, were kept in the file' (Fido 1977).

Others have traced subsequent twentieth-century developments in social work record-keeping and the varying styles that have been used. Timms describes four main phases of record-keeping, starting from pre-COS days:

1   the register type of record, which distinguishes the early nineteenth century and is little more than a brief one-line entry;
2   the more detailed diary type of entry to be found in the latter half of the nineteenth century and early twentieth century; records included key facts and the nature of the business transacted (sometimes in a 'behold-me-busy' style of writing);
3   the arrival of the 1930s style of process recording, whereby the writer records almost the totality of the interview with a view to professional analysis;
4   the differential record, combining process recording with strategic summaries of the case in order to make overall reading more manageable. (Timms 1972, pp. 8–16)

Timms was able to see an overlap between the different phases he had described, rather than definitive breaks. Even today, social workers might recognise the 'behold-me-busy' style of recording, and students sometimes still attempt process recording as part of their practice placement. A further trend identified by Timms was that of the visibility of files and records to the client. In the early days of the COS, records were clearly needed as evidence to decide if a person was deserving or undeserving, so there was no reason to hide the fact that notes were being taken and records kept. The shift in the 1930s to a more professional, therapeutic style of work relegated the record to a less visible position, often being completed after the 'real work' with the client had ended. This could well have led to dismissive attitudes towards records, in that they were not central to the social work project, but only a less valued 'mechanical extra' to be added on afterwards (Timms 1972, pp. 17–18). Today, this trend has arguably reversed, with a fifth phase which followed the introduction of access-to-files policies and the arrival of a new, more concise, minimalist form of record-keeping (see Chapter 5). In the late nineteenth century, such across the desk visibility reinforced the passive, dependent state of the client, in contrast to today's ideas of giving access and full sharing of files to enable empowerment of users (see, for example, Payne 1989; Beresford and Croft 1993).

The visibility of files may also have had some influence on their content. In the days before clients were allowed access, when files were the hidden-away accessories of social workers, there is much evidence to suggest that records were not kept very well. Although good examples must have existed, it is the poor quality of recording that repeatedly comes to the fore in what references there are on the subject. A Ministry of Health report at the end of the 1950s found that records 'tend to be poor or non-existent', and blamed pressure of work and lack of clerical support. The report also found that the value of records was not recognised (Ministry of Health 1959, para. 606).

Social work is seen as the 'real' work, to which writing up case records is an additional burden which amounts to nothing more than 'donkey-work'. The report into the death of Maria Colwell found that, although standards of recording were quite good, it was not a priority (DHSS 1974a, para. 153), and a DHSS project a few years later found similar views that recording was an 'unnecessary interference with the task of the social worker' (DHSS 1977, para. 26). Even the authorities seemed to send out ambivalent messages to their staff, giving little emphasis to recording and not much guidance on good practice (DHSS 1978a, para. 5.79).

Even in the increasingly high-profile work of child protection, evidence existed that there were 'problems and failures in preparing reports and records' (DHSS 1982, p. 50). The inquiry into the death of 4-year-old Paul Brown in Birkenhead found it quite 'disturbing' that 'if the case file had been fully written up and studied more closely the course of events might have been different' (DHSS 1980a, para. 103). The same message came through in the influential report into the death of Jasmine Beckford (London Borough of Brent 1985, pp. 223–34), and more generally in the findings of 'many examples of incomplete records' in a Department of Health summary of report findings (DoH 1991c, pp. 102–7). Behind these deficiencies lay the belief of many social workers that paperwork was not the same as social work (Shemmings 1991, p. 45).

Cohen found social services staff thought recording was 'an interference with their "real" job' (Cohen 1982, p. 45). Ovretveit reported that 'recording is viewed as a bureaucratic requirement with little to do with "real social work"' in his BASW-commissioned study (Ovretveit 1986, p. 11), and in his wider study of work orientations in a social work office, Pithouse found similar attitudes, even when access-to-files policies were coming into being:

> In [the social workers'] view their own day to day endeavours are the authentic realm of work and not their membership of a distanced department and the completion of their administrative requirements. 'Real work' is their face to face contact with service users. (Pithouse 1990, p. 48)

Various pressures have been brought to bear on social workers to persuade them to regard recording as a more integral part of their work. One of the dilemmas has always been whether management should enforce better record-keeping, or whether it should be an intrinsic part of being a professional social worker (see, for example, Cockburn 1990, pp. 56–7).

Reports suggest that social workers know they should prioritise record-keeping without being ordered to do so:

> in virtually all our studies social workers said their case notes were not up to date and expressed varying degrees of guilt and anxiety about this (DHSS 1978a, para. 5.75)

> as far as recording visits and events on case files was concerned, social workers knew that they were supposed to keep their files up to date. (Satyamurti 1981, 39)

By the 1990s, various external pressures were being brought to bear on social services recording. In the area of child protection, the requirements of courts and other agencies meant that better recording and report writing was needed on the part of social services staff. The opening up of files with access policies led to more careful recording, and the advent of information technology again focused minds on improving recording techniques.

Having convinced social workers that recording was a priority, and having got their records up to date, what might we expect to see in social services' files? What other kinds of record apart from the case-file need to be completed? In the remainder of this chapter we will explore the various forms of recording that take place in social services, from the basic case-file to registers, log books, video recording and other forms of storing and transmitting personal information.

Case records

The written case record – or manual file – has come to epitomise the nature of contemporary social work. The caseworker with his or her caseload represents the apotheosis of individualised casework – from the neatly-kept up-to-date case record to the bulging, sprawling out-of-date file that can hardly contain its dog-eared contents.

In 1983 the BASW added its voice to those who found case recording was too often a residual social work activity, which social workers felt constrained them, especially if they had to record in a format they felt had been imposed on them. Lack of time and other distractions led to case records being 'deficient as information systems' (BASW 1983, p. 6). On the one hand were short, incomplete records that confused fact with opinion, and on the other, over-written, verbose files that lacked basic information. Many examples of poor recording that mixed fact with opinion (and worse) can be found at this time. Cohen recalled seeing social work files which contained: 'information that was irrelevant, inaccurate and out-of-date ... files that were not dated at all and whose authors could not be identified ... [and files with] value-judgements, hearsay and gossip' (Cohen 1982, p. 76). Kinnibrugh examined 82 files in his study of case records and gave such examples as:

> Mrs. Knight is immature, looking years younger than her husband and is always well made up, looking like a 'dolly-bird' ... an agitated excitable woman ... despite this she appears mentally wide, crafty and doesn't miss a point.

> Mrs. O'Reilly presented as a very talkative and seemingly concerned mum. (Kinnibrugh 1984, pp. 121 and 124)

In my experience, the use of the word 'mum' or 'dad' by social services staff to describe parents is still widely in vogue in both the written and spoken word, despite its demeaning nature.

A constant complaint has been that clients become labelled through case records when opinions become confused with facts. Once such a label is affixed, it is very hard to shake off, and a gap can open up between the person as depicted on file and the person that exists in the flesh. Research from the USA even suggests that social workers unwittingly distort records to prove their case (Margolin 1992), and the power of language in social work generally is slowly being realised (Rojek et al. 1988); others have argued that therapeutic language and devices such as acronyms can disguise issues of power and control, even when no deliberate deceit is intended (Edelmann 1977; see also Cohen 1985, Appendix).

More recently, a report on the work of social services departments providing services for people living with HIV/AIDS found that 'case recording generally was not to a good standard' (SSI 1994b, para. 13.29) and that confidentiality was taken to extremes, perhaps to avoid stigma and labelling. Ultimately, this led to a 'too strict adherence to confidentiality, which worked against the interests of the service users and carers' (para. 13.27), even to the extent of social workers not keeping any records at all when service users refused them permission to do so (para. 13.10).

In the BASW's opinion in the early 1980s, nothing less than a 'radical reappraisal' of the role and organisation of case recording was needed (BASW 1983, p. 8). The BASW saw it as a priority that case records should be accurate and easily kept up to date, and be easy to retrieve. Their main objective should be to provide records and information necessary for the best possible service to be given to the user. Mostly, the records should contain facts or material that is verifiable, alongside more subjective judgements and assessments. Room was also to be found for straight narrative and observations (BASW 1983, 15). The BASW outlined ten major uses for a case record:

1   for management control, to provide as good a service as possible;
2   to provide continuity of service between individual workers;
3   for self-justification, although they recognised the need to still be con-
    cise;
4   for legal purposes; then, and even more so now, numerous legal re-
    quirements have been placed on social services staff to keep written
    records;
5   for work support, and to clarify thinking; the BASW believed that
    'clinical musings' – speculation on possible different courses of action –
    should be kept separate;
6   for supervision and teaching, although it was felt undesirable to depart
    from 'normal' case recording undertaken in an agency;
7   for purposes of information storage, which should none the less be
    limited and not excessive;
8   for personal evaluation, although the BASW believed this only proved
    that workers could write records;
9   for planning, research, financial control and agency evaluation, pur-
    poses which were not necessarily compatible with a good personal
    information recording and retrieval system;
10 for personal identity, to record facts about a service user's life which
    they might wish to have access to in later life. (BASW 1983, Chapter 3)

The BASW did not necessarily commend these ten uses, but recognised
them as being the basis of most contemporary recording systems in social
services. They further believed that information storage (item 7) should
have a policy of retention attached to it, and that really detailed recording
in child protection and similar work, could be kept separately. The self-
justification use (item 3) should never develop into the belief that 'if it's not
on record, you didn't do it'.

Reporting in 1983, the BASW was unaware of the way in which social
workers would become less producers of records and information for their
own purposes and more producers of information for other people. In child
protection work in particular, a shift from a socio-medical perspective to a
socio-legal perspective in the latter part of the 1980s turned social workers
more than ever into major producers of personal information and 'social
knowledge' for the police, various agencies in child protection conferences
and related work, and the courts. This movement has been commented on
by Parton:

the type of 'evidence' and the form of expertise which is most vital in helping
courts make such sensitive decisions is to be derived more than any other from
social work. Not only will it be local authority social workers who will apply for
Emergency Protection Orders, Child Assessment Orders and Care Orders, but

the independent experts who the courts will draw upon for their advice in the guise of guardians ad litem will also be social workers. (Parton 1991, p. 213)

The traditional purpose of 'domestic' record-keeping – to enable social workers to do the job and justify their work – is now augmented by the keeping of records and production of personal information for other people, in the form of reports to court and conference minutes to be shared with other agencies. Even before a child protection conference starts, there is an expectation that written reports will be submitted to all:

> investigating officers and key workers, in particular, should prepare thoroughly and will normally provide written reports covering both past and present incidents of abuse, information about the family circumstances, details of work undertaken and proposals for the future. Other professional workers should be encouraged to have available at the conference other written reports to which they can refer. (Home Office et al. 1991, para. 6.33)

In legal terms, the Children Act 1989 and its accompanying regulations placed statutory requirements on social services staff to produce a whole array of written reports and records, not just for child protection work, but for all areas of child care. In part this was to keep parents and other professionals informed, and in part it was an exercise in greater accountability. It was also another avenue for social workers to interpret and provide information for a wider audience. (Table 3.1 includes all the legal references – for example, requiring written records when a child is placed with foster-parents.)

The same pattern can be noted in areas of social work unrelated to child protection. The social services provision of youth justice services has seen the production of information for inter-agency panels deciding on cautions or prosecution (Thomas 1994a, pp. 115–24), and for the courts in the form of pre-sentence reports (Gibson et al. 1994, Chapter 6). The courts also receive information from social services to help them make decisions on remands (Gibson et al. 1994, Chapter 7). Elsewhere, hospitals may expect social history reports on some of their patients, and if social workers are involved with mentally disordered offenders, information reports may again be needed for the courts, mental health review tribunals, the police and other agencies. 'Restricted patients' within the meaning of the Mental Health Act 1983 (Sections 37 and 47) must have reports on them sent regularly to the Home Office (Home Office/DHSS 1987, para. 50).

Other formal channels could be cited whereby social services staff have become producers of 'social knowledge' for other people. Community care arrangements are dependent on a free flow of personal information. The demands of various registers for personal information will be considered in the next section. All of these formal channels are supplemented by informal

Table 3.1   Legal requirements to keep written records in relation to children placed with foster-parents

Arrangements for Placement of Children (General) Regulations, SI 1991 No. 890

- Arrangements for the placement of a child in foster care 'shall be recorded in writing' (Regulation 3(5)).
- There must be 'a written case record' of each child placed (Regulation 1).

Foster Placement (Children) Regulations, SI 1991 No. 910

- Notice of approval must be given to an approved foster-parent (Regulation 3(6)(a)).
- A 'written agreement' must be drawn up before a child is placed with a foster-parent (the Foster Care Agreement) (Regulation 3(6)(b)).
- Reviews of 'approval' of foster-parents must be prepared as a report (Regulation 493).
- A written agreement (the Placement Agreement) must be drawn up before a child is placed (Regulation 5(6); Schedule 3).
- A written report is required on all formal visits to a foster-child (Regulation 6(4)).
- Special written agreements are required for emergency foster placements (Regulation 11(3)(b)).
- Records must be kept on each approved foster-parent (Regulation 13(1)).

Contact with Children Regulations, SI 1991 No. 891

- Any refusal of contact with a child must be put in writing to those who need to know (Regulation 2).
- A local authority's departure from a court order on contact must be put in writing to those who need to know (Regulation 3).
- Any variation or suspension of contact arrangements must be put in writing to those who need to know (Regulation 4).

Review of Children's Cases Regulations, SI 1991 No. 895

- Review arrangements should be 'set out in writing' (Regulation 4(1)).
- A written assessment of a child's health must be kept (Regulation 6).
- Reviews and decisions must be 'recorded in writing' (Regulation 10).

Representations Procedure (Children) Regulations, SI 1991 No. 894

- Oral complaints and representations must be 'accurately recorded in writing' (Regulation 4(2)).
- Complaints from non-relatives declaring an interest may be turned down, but the complainant must be notified 'in writing' (Regulation 4(4)(c)).
- Notice of the results of a complaint having been considered must be sent to interested parties (Regulation 8(1)).
- The result must be recorded with 'reasons in writing' (Regulation 9(1)).

networks whereby social services staff are in constant communication with a range of other practitioners and agencies to supply either 'raw' personal information or personal information with added social work expertise to interpret it. Either way, we have moved into an era of social services storing personal information not just for their own work purposes, but as 'information managers' for the wider community.

In 1983, the BASW might also have been unaware of the full extent of other changes that would take place, such as access-to-files policies and the introduction of more concise recording, and the advent of information technology. The BASW did see the need for the case record to be kept in a strong manila outer cover with front sheets storing basic information, an initial summary of 'presenting problems' at referral and a running chronological narrative, with each entry dated and legibly signed. Periodic summaries, letters and correspondence should be kept separately on file, along with such documents as pre-sentence reports, and legal documents like Supervision Orders or Care Orders. The BASW was not the only organisation attempt to give guidance on good record-keeping (see, for example, DHSS 1977; Kinnibrugh 1984, pp. 98–106).

Registers

Registers have become a favoured device in social services work for storing personal information. An initial list of names can be the key to further files of more detailed personal information. The rationale for registers can vary from the local need to improve service delivery and inter-agency work to the national registers, to which social workers contribute to provide statistical information and help resource-allocation exercises. Some registers are kept locally but also serve a national purpose.

Possibly the best-known registers are the Child Protection Registers that have been kept by local authorities since the early 1970s and were put on a formal footing following the Maria Colwell inquiry (DHSS 1974a). This inquiry into the death of a 7-year-old child became a watershed in thinking about child abuse in the UK. Registers were to be part of the co-ordinated response to try to minimise the risks to children posed by their carers (DHSS 1974b). A child discussed at a child protection conference could have his or her name put on the register, and any agencies coming across suspicious incidents involving children could consult the register to see if the child was already known. Subsequent circulars and guidance have further codified the nature of the Child Protection Registers (DHSS 1980b; Home Office et al. 1991, paras 6.36–6.54). In the jointly-produced guidance, the Department of Health now suggests registers should:

list all the children in the area who are considered to be suffering from or likely
to suffer significant harm and for whom there is a child protection plan …
children for whom there are currently unresolved child protection issues. (Home
Office et al. 1991, para. 6.36)

Children are categorised in terms of the abuse they have suffered or seem
likely to suffer: neglect, physical injury, sexual abuse and emotional abuse
(para. 6.40). A fifth category of 'grave concern', covering children who did
not fit into the other four, was phased out with the implementation of the
Children Act 1989 in October 1991; it had become vague in interpretation,
and this varied from one area to another. The number of children on the
register in England on 31 March 1993 was approximately 32,500, which was
evidence of a steady fall from a high of 45,300 in 1991 (see DoH 1994a).

Registers have been criticised for being expensive, bureaucratic and irrelevant (Morris et al. 1980, pp. 118–21). As with any data bank of personal
information, they run the risk of being accused of being a threat to civil
liberties. Agencies seeking information from a register may or may not treat
the information as confidential, and sometimes even phone-back systems
by the custodians of registers to ensure the bona fides of enquirers have not
always been adhered to.

Even more worrying have been cases where information from a register
has been given to people who have not asked for it. We examine the details
of one such case in Chapter 4 (see pages 87–8), but suffice to say here that
the judge described the Child Protection Register in that case as 'having
dangerous potential as an instrument of injustice or oppression' (*R* v. *Norfolk CC ex parte M* [1989] 2 All ER 359).

From time to time, recommendations have been made that a national
child protection register be created to complement the present local systems
(see, for example, London Borough of Greenwich 1987, pp. 156–8; London
Borough of Lambeth 1987, p. 101). At present, families on a local register
who move and whose whereabouts are unknown may be traced either by
sending a standard letter to all other local authorities to ask if they have
come across the family or, if more serious, tracking the family down through
the social security system. Details of this system of tracking through the
Department of Social Security were contained in a confidential letter from
the then Chief Social Work Officer of the DHSS to all directors of social
services, dated 29 March 1977 (see DHSS 1980b, para. 4.13).

Child Protection Registers are focused on children, but their information
systems also contain the names of adults living in a household in order to
identify possible perpetrators of abuse. Some local authorities also maintain registers of convicted adults living in an area who are known to have
offended against children (Home Office et al. 1991, paras 6.52–6.54).

Local authorities who keep local criminal record systems of adult child
abusers are effectively only duplicating national systems, and in particular

the national collection of criminal records. To all intents and purposes, this national collection held by the police is simply another massive register with some 5.5 million names on it. When it was originally created it was known as the Habitual Criminals Register (Habitual Criminals Act 1869). Today, social services departments have daily access to it, through the police, for child protection purposes. The police disclose information at child protection conferences and in writing on receipt of formal requests for vetting childminders, foster-parents and others. The Home Office estimated that around 665,000 child protection disclosures were made to local authorities in the year ending 31 March 1993, an increase of 23 per cent on the previous year (Home Office 1993, para. 23). In West Yorkshire alone, for example, 20,000 child protection disclosures were made in 1992 (West Yorkshire Chief Constable's Annual Report 1992, p. 51).

Social services departments using previous conviction records are essentially filtering out those convictions that concern children and which are generally referred to as 'Schedule 1 offences'. This is a reference to Schedule 1 of the Children and Young Persons Act 1933, which lists all the offences it is possible to commit against children. Researchers at the University of Manchester believe that, when it comes to child sexual abuse, there is still 'no way of tracking perpetrators as they move around the country' (Hughes and Parker 1994), and that a national register of sex abusers is still needed ('Child Sex Abuse "is widespread"', *The Times*, 18 June 1994).

In 1990 the Metropolitan Police created a national database of known paedophiles (Culf 1990), and in 1992 the database was incorporated into the work of the newly-created National Criminal Intelligence Service (NCIS). Today the paedophile index, which is thought to have had a limited impact, is part of the Specialist Crime Unit within the NCIS Strategic and Specialist Intelligence Branch (NCIS 1994). According to some reports, the low level of use of the database 'brings into question knowledge of the unit's existence among provincial forces' (Hyder and Rose 1994).

Moving away from child protection issues as such, social services also keep registers of approved childminders, play groups, out-of-school clubs and day nurseries (Children Act 1989, Section 71). Information on the register should include 'name, address, telephone number and number of places' (DoH 1991d, para. 7.47(b)).

Children placed in foster-care by a local authority may only be placed with foster-parents who have been approved and placed on a register (Foster Placement (Children) Regulations 1991, SI 1991 No. 910, Regulation 12), and the placement itself, when it takes place, will also find itself on its own register, whether inside or outside the authority's area (Arrangements for Placement of Children (General) Regulations 1991, SI 1991 No. 890, Regulation 10). The latter register will 'provide a means of immediate reference to basic information about any child placed in an area' (DoH 1991e, para. 2.80).

Proprietors of private children's homes must be approved and registered, as must proprietors of private care homes for elderly people (Registered Homes Act 1984, Sections 1 and 5).

Disabled children in a given locality are recorded on a register to improve service planning and monitoring (Children Act 1989, Schedule 2, para. 2). The register could be shared by social services, education and health authorities (DoH 1991f, para. 4.2–4.3). Disabled adults are registered by social services in their own right, in accordance with the Chronically Sick and Disabled Persons Act 1970, Section 1, and by the employment service in terms of the Disabled Persons (Employment) Acts 1944 and 1958.

Disabled people who are blind or partially sighted may also find themselves on a register maintained by social services departments under Section 29(4)(g) of the National Assistance Act 1948. For people to be registered, a consultant opthalmologist must examine them and complete the standard reporting form BD8. The Department of Health collates national statistics from the local Register of Blind and Partially Sighted Persons on a triennial basis (DoH 1991g).

Similar Registers of the Deaf and Hard of Hearing are maintained under the same legal authority of the National Assistance Act. There are no formal examination procedures for inclusion on the register other than completion of form SSDA910 by a social services department officer (DoH 1992).

Registers have been proposed to help keep information on former mental health hospital in-patients. Of particular concern has been the after-care of people who might be considered dangerous. After Jonathan Zito was killed by Christopher Clunis, a mentally disordered man, in December 1992, the ensuing inquiry report recommended two new registers be created: one to be held by the Mental Health Act Commission and to consist of Section 117 plans (named after the Mental Health Act 1983, Section 117, which places a duty on local authorities to provide after-care services to anyone formerly detained under the Act), and the other, also to be nationally held, of all those former patients designated as part of a Special Supervision Group (detained more than once, homeless, with history of violence and offending, etc.). Together, the Section 117 Register and the Supervision Register were to assist in the community care management of former patients considered to be particularly problematic (NE Thames and SE Thames Regional Health Authorities 1994, paras 45.2.3 and 47.0.15(iii)).

Registers for former mental health hospital in-patients had been on various agendas before the Clunis case (see, for example, House of Commons 1985, para. 219). An inquiry following the death of a social worker at the hands of a mentally ill person had proposed the need for registers (DHSS 1988a, para. 16.21). Some *ad hoc* registers have been created in some areas and been roundly criticised for this infringement of civil liberties (Sayce 1991). The Clunis Report dismissed such fears, saying: 'the benefits of a

Register far outweigh any concerns' (NE Thames and SE Thames Regional Health Authorities 1994, para. 47.0.14).

The Department of Health responded to concerns with its 'ten-point plan' for the supervised discharge of psychiatric patients (DoH Press Release, 12 August 1993) and went on to publish administrative arrangements on how local Supervision Registers might work; so far they have not been persuaded on the need for Section 117 Registers. The Supervision Register was seen as listing three categories of people: those at risk of self-harm, those who might harm others, and those at risk of severe self-neglect. The register would enable swift identification, assessment of the nature of risk and identification of key workers and relevant professionals, and would give information on the care programme (NHS Management Executive 1994).

Supervision Registers have been criticised as being stigmatising, infringing civil liberties and as being ineffective (AMA 1994). MIND has questioned their legality and whether or not they infringe Article 8 of the European Convention on Human Rights. They also suggest the £77 million estimated cost of setting up and maintaining registers could be better spent on direct provision of community care services (MIND 1994a and 1994b). On the other hand, the Data Protection Registrar has cast an eye over them and pronounced them satisfactory if suitable safeguards are built in (DPR 1994, p. 13). Health professionals were seen as the prime holders of the registers, but social workers would have access as part of the 'care network' (see also DoH 1994b).

The movement towards registers sometimes seems to have a momentum of its own. Registers of elderly people at risk from carers and others have been proposed (Murray 1993), although a Law Commission report into various problems experienced by mentally incapacitated and other vulnerable adults did not commit itself on the idea (Law Commission 1993). Registers of private domicilary care services have been suggested as another means of protecting elderly people, and the Association of Directors of Social Services lobbied to have this form of registration included in the NHS and Community Care Act 1990. Similar registers have been suggested for those working in private residential care (Fry 1993). It has also been suggested that a national register be kept of all the UK's 35,000 nannies (Working Mothers Association 1992) and even of all clients/service users known to have been violent toward social services staff or to have made threats, in order that an appropriate response be made to them in the interests of worker safety (Norris 1990, p. 161). Women who have been victims of violence in their own homes have been put forward as another example of where registers might help to enable a faster police response (see Travis 1990).

Within the statutory social services world itself, the idea of registering those practitioners allowed to work in the welfare field has been put forward. A general social services council has been suggested to cover all those engaged in providing local social services, and this council would be custodian of a register. The Parker Report thought the arguments were 'compelling', and considered a range of issues concerning mandatory or non-mandatory registration and how pre-registration periods might work (Parker 1990, pp. 101ff). If achieved, such arrangements would presumably supersede the present 'negative register' held by the Department of Health as its Consultancy Service, maintaining a list of some 6,000 people who are considered *not* fit to work in social services (see *Hansard* 23 October 1989 PQ 4982–5; Home Office 1993b, Annex C).

The use of registers to record personal information in social services is widespread, and we have listed only the main ones here. It almost seems that recourse to registers is something of a UK tradition, but perhaps it is part of a wider tradition in modern Western societies to try to create a sense of order out of that which is potentially disordered.

If a register gives a sense of order and a potential means of identification of people, it allows more certainty and reliability to be brought into service delivery and planning, pinning down the 'city of strangers'. In terms of protecting people from various forms of risk, the idea of the register is less promising. It may seem to offer certainty and reliability, but it remains true that inclusion on a register in itself has never protected anyone, and the illusion is shattered every time a child on a Child Protection Register is killed (see Hearn 1991).

Audio recording

Audio recording takes place in social services work, and the resulting tapes constitute a record of personal information. Tapes can be made of interviews in order to facilitate later analysis, and may be used in student social work education as learning material. The consent of the person being interviewed should be obtained, and covert taping or taping of telephone conversations would be considered unethical, even if not illegal if the person is doing it to their own telephone (Chamberlain 1987).

Video recording

The use of video recording in social services work has possibly outstripped that of audio-taping. Its use has grown as the technology has developed, and can now be found in anything from family therapy work, possibly using two-way mirrors, to social skills training with young offenders or people with learning difficulties through to 'advertising' children in need of foster-carers. However, it is in the field of child protection work that we have seen the greatest increase in the use of video technology.

Since the law was changed to permit the use of video-taped interviews with children in court hearings, the recording of such interviews has become standard practice (Criminal Justice Act 1988, Section 32, as amended). The aim is to protect the child from the ordeal of the court and possibly facing his or her abuser, and to prevent the child having to repeat his or her story to different professionals. The Home Office and Department of Health have jointly issued guidance on the best way to carry out video interviews (Home Office/DoH 1992).

Once the video recording is in existence, it comprises yet another form of personal information record, containing 'intimate personal information and images [which] should be held strictly in confidence and for its proper purpose' (Home Office/DoH, para. 4.2). Any video tape stored by social services, whether for child protection purposes or any other, is to be accorded the same degree of confidentiality as a written record (DoH 1988, para. 3), child protection interview tapes should 'never be left lying about' (Home Office/DoH 1992, para. 4.10) and all their movements must be carefully logged. The police are considered the best agency to keep them, and all tapes should be destroyed when no longer needed (para. 4.15).

Video-taped interviews of children are now carried out jointly by police and social workers. Sometimes they are carried out in a 'grossly inadequate' manner (see, for example, *Re A and Others (Minors)* [1992] 1 FLR 439), and they are often not used in any court proceedings ('In the frame', *Community Care*, 28 October 1993).

Video tapes may also come into the possession of the social services department when the technique known as covert video surveillance (CVS) has been used. CVS is usually carried out on hospital premises to secretly record visiting parents interacting with their children who are in a hospital bed. The aim of the exercise is to seek evidence of abusive behaviour towards a child. A special surveillance cubicle is set up with concealed cameras, and with nurses on hand to observe and intervene should the child be in danger. Social services should be involved in the initial decision to use CVS, and the resulting tapes may be used by social services if care proceedings are entered into.

CVS was first reported to have been used in the UK at the Royal Brompton Hospital in London in the mid-1980s, and the technique has subsequently been developed and refined. It is used particularly to help identify children thought to have experienced abuse from those suffering Munchausen's syndrome by proxy, a condition whereby the sufferers deliberately injure others in order to gain attention from medical professionals.

The use of CVS has been criticised as an invasion of privacy and a breach of trust between doctors and patients (see, for example, Foreman and

Farsides 1993). *The Lancet* felt that 'the concept of permanently bugged cubicles … is surely unacceptable' ('Diagnosing recurrent suffocation of children', *The Lancet*, 1992, No. 340, p. 87) and the whole process 'a waste of time, money and professional effort' ('Spying on mothers', *The Lancet*, 1994, No. 343, pp. 1,373–4). Others have even suggested that the term 'Munchausen's syndrome by proxy' is nothing more than a 'fake disease' and, until better defined, 'should be abandoned' (*ibid.*; see also Morgan 1994); towards the end of 1994 a group of parents reportedly intended to sue doctors for using 'unproven techniques' and making false accusations against them (Lightfoot 1994).

Despite these criticisms, CVS continues to be used, and a protocol on how it can best be managed has been produced by Staffordshire Area Child Protection Committee (Staffordshire ACPC 1994). This protocol has been commended by the Department of Health, who suggest any authorities thinking of carrying out CVS should follow it (*Children Act News*, No. 12, February 1994, p. 5). When asked a parliamentary question on whether or not the Department of Health had its own plans to regulate CVS, however, the junior minister completely misunderstood the question and thought it referred to security cameras in hospital corridors and car parks (*Hansard*, 24 October 1994, PQ 5469; see also Thomas 1994b and 1994c).

Oral records

The spoken word is an easily overlooked major repository of personal information in social services departments. Information is exchanged with numerous other professionals and in forums such as child protection conferences and other meetings, youth justice panels, co-working and joint investigative work in child protection. The amount of information exchanged in this manner is almost limitless.

The point at issue here is whether we can define the spoken word as another form of personal information record-keeping. Some discussions will become formal written records, as when meetings are minuted; others will not. There is always the tension between what people recall they said and what appears on paper. Unspoken body language will rarely be recorded in written form. Inevitably, the spoken word is less certain and more transitory compared to the written, permanent record. It is perhaps worth noting that a DES consultative document on record-keeping in schools suggested that conversations between two members of staff about a school pupil did effectively constitute a record (DES 1988a, para. 5).

However, the spoken word in 'private' between colleagues may also be a means of 'sounding off' and relaxing from normal, formal interchanges. It may be replete with obscenities, exaggerations and other light-hearted comments that are 'off the record', 'not for public consumption' and are not intended to be malicious. Overheard, they could be misconstrued.

The spoken word is possibly more important in residential care work, where messages and communications are often oral and face-to-face. The difficulties of recalling and establishing what was really said may contribute as much as anything to the pressures of working in residential care.

In terms of the security and confidentiality of personal information, the spoken word is the easiest way for information to be disclosed. An experiment in the mid-1970s revealed how easily social work offices gave out information over the telephone to callers they did not know (Brandon 1975).

As for deliberately listening in on private conversations, the quaint old practice of eavesdropping was declared not to be a crime by the Criminal Law Act 1967, Section 13. Moreover, it would not be an offence for a client to secretly tape record a telephone conversation with his or her social worker if the telephone was their own.

Day books and log books

A form of recording found in residential and day services settings more than fieldwork settings is the use of the day book or log book to record events in a diary fashion to enable changing shifts of workers to maintain continuity in their activities. Both residential and day service settings have over the years employed less qualified workers than the fieldwork side of social services, and the poor quality of day and log book recording has reflected this.

An extreme case study of poor recording in log books was revealed in the report of the inquiry into the 'Pindown' affair in Staffordshire Social Services. Although primarily concerned with the abusive regime found in residential child care in Staffordshire, the report reproduced verbatim some log book entries that were both judgemental and unprofessional. Children were described as 'high as a kite' (Levy and Kahan 1991, para. 4.32) and in such derogatory terms as: '[she] must work her short and curlies off and not stop till she drops' (para. 8.38), and 'she thinks I'm room service, hasn't anyone told her it's not a hotel ... when I go in I usually look for a tip as I feel like a waiter' (para. 11.24).

No doubt good examples of log book recording do exist, but the Department of Health has gone out of its way to give guidance that records in residential child care should be 'factual, accurate and clear' and not include 'gratuitous value judgements', 'colloquialisms' or stigmatising terms (DoH 1991b, para. 1.160).

Statutory regulations advise on the information to be recorded on children in children's homes (DoH 1991b, Schedule 2) and on what other records need to be kept, including log books, accident records, menu records and records of disciplinary measures (Schedule 3). Despite this guidance, a survey of 93 authorities revealed that 25 of them had still not passed suitable guidance to staff employed in children's homes on the substance of good practice in log book and diary recording (DoH 1993c, para. 5.17). An inspection report on the homes of one authority found information was not always stored in the appropriate section of the file, and described some files as so chaotic as to be 'nothing more than a receptacle for papers' (SSI 1993a, pp. 61–2).

Computer records

Social work and social services generally have been slow in coming to terms with information technology. This was only remedied in recent years, and not least with the advent of new community care arrangements. The idea – if not the practice – of using information technology in social services has been around for quite a while. In 1968 the Local Authorities Management Services and Computer Committee (LAMSAC) was created, with its own social services applications sub-group concerned with the effective use of computers in social services departments. Initial attempts to computerise departments started in the mid-1970s, using centralised mainframe computers. Social workers were called on to complete endless forms to keep the computer up to date, and many systems foundered in the process. The 1978 Lindop Committee·of inquiry into computer use found that 'so little sensitive social work information is computerised' that a right of access was hardly worth having (Lindop Report 1978, para. 24.10).

In addition to the limitations of the cumbersome technology, there was a belief amongst some social services staff that the very idea of computerised information, and its accompanying ethos of industry and commerce, was somehow alien to working with people. The complexities of family dynamics and human relationships were not suitable for processing through the narrow view of the computer, and no doubt added to this belief was an extension of the argument that saw recording generally as not 'real social work'. One observer lamented that:

> Social workers have not been in the vanguard of demands for computer applications – there has only been a small group of people hitting their heads on a brick wall, not being able to persuade their colleagues that there's anything in it. (cited in Morris 1987)

Some social workers also saw the 'Big Brother' analogy: that computers somehow made you a more powerful agent and one that could induce more social control (Powell 1980). The loss of confidentiality was proclaimed in alarmist headlines such as: 'Police share computer with social services' (*Childright*, 1983, No. 2, p. 6). The situation began to change with the Data Protection Act 1984. LAMSAC produced its Code of Practice (Pearse et al. 1988, pp. 56–79), and the BASW formed its Data Protection Advisory Panel (see, for example, BASW 1982).

The arrival of the micro-chip and the personal computer replacing the mainframe computer introduced a new era of accessibility and flexibility (Glastonbury 1985; Turnbull 1986). Suggestions even surfaced that computers could take over some of the tasks of the social worker, and at the very least support him or her in making social work decisions: a computer program might help make decisions in child protection work, for example (Algie 1986), or help make the decision on when people should be discharged from a psychiatric hospital (Davidson 1991). The computer seemed super-human, offering certainty and precision in an uncertain world.

Applications in social services started at a less ambitious level, with indexes, names and addresses and registers. A movement to case record systems has been slower to arrive: 'This is the essential first step for further developments … what currently goes into a folder – forms, reports, notes, reviews, all of it – is entered through a keyboard and stored on a small floppy disc' (Glastonbury 1985, p. 114). LAMSAC pioneered the Client Records Information and Social Services package (CRISP), and the private sector came forward with a succession of new applications (Hardingham 1986). A new journal appeared called *Computer Applications in Social Work*, later to be renamed *New Technology in the Human Services*, and technology and its accompanying ethical problems moved forward together.

On a pragmatic level, social services had to draw up security guidelines and procedures, often the responsibility of an appointed member of staff. Equipment had to be sited in secure locations not vulnerable to vandalism or theft, and with video display units placed where they could not be seen by members of the public. Discs had to be stored securely, and passwords created to gain access to computer files. Back-up procedures had to be established to ensure data could be recovered in the event of accidental loss or damage. A major push forward for computer applications in social services came with the arrival of new ways of delivering care in the community following the NHS and Community Care Act 1990. The moves were part of a generally changing culture among local authorities which, in social services terms, was to take departments away from the traditional, integrated direct service department to a more devolved system of purchasing services from various providers.

Integral to the changes was a need for information technology to assist the devolution of managerial and financial responsibility and the new roles of social services closer to the service users and more directly accountable through devolved budgets. Everyone was suddenly on an upward learning curve that accepted no resistance and no rigid thinking or 'mind-fix' to hold developments back. The metaphor of the central nervous system was employed as information technology penetrated throughout social services departments and computers took on the work of both storing and communicating personal information. The computer had arrived and was no longer just a 'dumb' desk accessory to make a manager look important.

4 Regulating information privacy in social services

In Chapter 1 we pictured personal information as something that emanates from a person or confidential communication between two people and then goes into wider circulation. Normally, someone has given consent to this circulation, and it takes place with that person's interests at heart. If, on the other hand, consent has not been given, or it has been qualified consent, how can the circulation of that personal information be policed or regulated to ensure a degree of information privacy? What sanctions can be brought to apply if regulation is failing or has failed? The late Paul Sieghart neatly summarised the problem:

> You try to ensure that the right people always get the right information for the right purposes, but that the wrong people do not, and that the information is not wrong and that it does not get misused for wrong purposes. (Sieghart 1983)

One way to represent the regulation of personal information flows in social services is to imagine a series of bands surrounding the individual or family that is the source of the information. Three primary bands of professional, administrative and legal regulation exist, and within those three bands various sub-sections can be defined. This can be represented in diagrammatic form (see Figure 4.1).

In the first band, at the point closest to the subject of the personal information, circulation is contained within a professional relationship, and often simply within the dyad of the worker and user of the service. Professional regulation is the starting point for policing the movement of personal information, and this in turn is reinforced by the next band of administrative regulation imposed by the organisation and bureaucracy which employs the professional worker. The professional is wrapped around by procedures, codes of guidance and administrative directions. Finally, we move

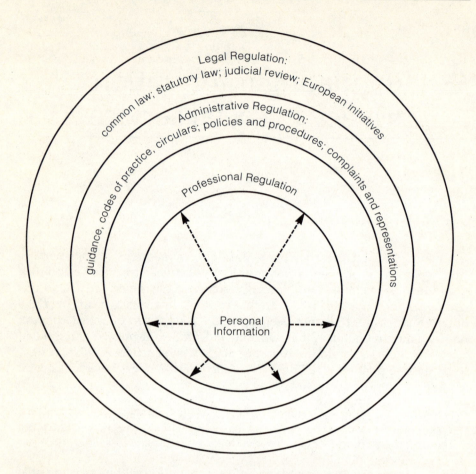

Figure 4.1   The regulation of personal information movement

out to the third band, which offers legal regulation to the agency and its workers and is nationally imposed, applicable to all citizens and agencies operating within its jurisdiction.

Regulation normally supposes that there has been no consent to this personal information flow or that there has been qualified consent. At times, regulation may be needed even if there has been consent.

Consent

The problems of regulation are lessened if people have consented to the disclosure of personal information about themselves, but as we shall see, there can be times when consent is dispensed with, and then regulation assumes a more important role.

Consent itself is not a straightforward concept, as we saw in Chapter 2 (see pages 20–21). How much information on the consequences of disclosure should a person be given, for example, in order to give 'informed' or 'real' consent? How much do they reflect on and appreciate that information? How much real or imagined duress are they under which clouds their judgement? How much of a Hobson's choice do they think they have, so that they really have no choice but to consent because the information will be disclosed anyway?

Consent can be broken down along a continuum from whole-hearted, 'real' consent at one end, to reluctant, submissive consent at the other. Social workers at one end of the spectrum could be accused of engineering consent through a process of selective advice, 'coercive persuasion' or even veiled threats (see Forbes and Thomas 1989). If consent means anything, it means that social workers may have to accept at times that people will not wish to give consent however much it may appear to the worker in their interests to do so. If it is withheld, social workers should honour that decision.

Consent may also be problematic when working with certain categories of people receiving social services. Children, for example, may not be competent to give reasoned consent, although the Children's Legal Centre has suggested they should at least be consulted when their personal information is circulated (CLC 1988, p. 10). The official solicitor acting on behalf of the children in the Cleveland Inquiry made the same point (Official Solicitor 1988, p. 119). How far children are competent to make these sort of decisions requires a fine assessment in keeping with the Gillick judgment. This judgment and the difficulty of children's consent are considered further in Chapter 5, where the same questions arise (see page 101; see also page 80).

People with learning difficulties or other incapacities may also have little understanding of the nature of consent and what the consequences of consenting to personal information disclosure might be. Other difficulties might arise with people whose first language is not English, and appropriate steps – such as providing interpreters – would need to be taken to gain their 'real' consent.

It has also been suggested that thinking about consent might be more focused if that consent was written rather than verbal. Kagle in the USA has proposed an authorisation for the release of information form, completed in triplicate by the service users or their guardians, the parties disclosing and the parties receiving the information. The form would contain a description of the information to be released and how it would be used, as well as the signatures of the three parties concerned (Kagle 1991, p. 139); the idea has also been considered in the UK (see, for example, Kinnibrugh 1984, p. 32).

Disclosure without consent forms the basis for breach of confidence actions, as we shall see. In statutory law we might also note that the third principle of data protection in the Data Protection Act 1984, with respect to computer-held information, does not allow the disclosure of information collected for one purpose to be used for another. If it is so disclosed, a person could seek compensation if his or her authority had not been given for the disclosure (Data Protection Act 1984, Section 23(1)(c)). It would seem that anyone trying to claim such compensation would be facing an uphill struggle and at the time of writing no one is believed to have attempted it in relation to social services.

Whether or not consent is written down or enshrined in statute, the point is that it is not a straightforward decision, and it varies with the capacity of the person making it and also with the nature of the consent sought. At the end of the day it may even be useful to think in terms of 'negotiated consent' that takes place between worker and client to decide on what should be disclosed and what kept confidential (see, for example, Thompson 1979).

Professional regulation

As social work has striven over the years to achieve professional status, so it has sought to regulate its own concept of confidentiality. An obligation of confidence arises when one person passes personal information to another expecting that it will be kept confidential. Post-war writers on social work believed that confidentiality is 'fundamental to professional relationships' (Ministry of Health 1959, para. 1,090), and:

> the caseworker has an ethical obligation, arising from the implicit contract, to keep the confidence. Social workers have had no need to theorise about the nature of the ethical obligation, because their consciousness of being professional persons always inclined them to accept confidentiality wholeheartedly. (Biestek 1961, p. 124)

Today it is implicit in all social services work that confidentiality of information is, in theory at least, a central tenet of the job. There is an expectation that education and training in social work will at some point focus on the need to preserve confidentiality. Students completing the Diploma in Social Work must demonstrate an ability to respect people's 'privacy and confidentiality' (CCETSW 1991a, para. 2.2.2), and in terms of skills required, must be able to 'record, accurately and succinctly [and] carry out agency policy in relation to confidentiality and subject access' (para. 2.3.4).

Practice placements and academic studies in the Diploma in Social Work programme will assess the students' competency to understand when personal information is to be held in confidence and when it may be properly disclosed. It has to be said, at the end of such a period of studies there is little formal acknowledgement that a student is now entering a profession that has certain commitments towards an ethical base that includes upholding the value of confidentiality: nothing, for example, comparable to the Hippocratic oath of the new doctor which, amongst other things, demands that personal information 'which ought not to be spread abroad, I will keep secret and never reveal'. None the less a notion of confidentiality is passed on to the newly-qualified worker.

Confidentiality can be distorted within a working context when it is restricted to keeping professional exchanges confidential. Although at times this may be necessary, on a regular basis this form of confidentiality amounts to secrecy when a professional grouping would really rather not share information with anyone else. At worst, it is the ubiquitous 'cover-up' and closing of ranks when things have gone wrong.

The London Borough of Kingston upon Thames Social Services Department were accused by a court of: 'an over zealous insistence on confidentiality in failing to tell the plaintiff what had happened to her' (*Surtees* v. *Kingston upon Thames Royal Borough Council, The Times* Law Report, 16 May 1989). If confidentiality means keeping in confidence that which is disclosed to you by a client, then, in this instance, the court was referring to a form of departmental secrecy, rather than confidentiality as we have come to know it.

Social workers have also been accused of holding back information to which people are entitled in order to make their task easier. Most notorious has been the accusation that information on children has been withheld in order to facilitate adoptions that take children out of care. One alleged victim of this practice said she 'could form a club from the number of well-meaning, innocent adopters who were duped by social workers trying to get another one off the books' (Henderson 1994). Research studies appear to bear out these allegations, with as many as one-third of fostering and adoptive parents having no knowledge, for example, of a child's previous sexual abuse (Ward 1993).

Social services departments with workers involved with people living with HIV and AIDS have also been reportedly over-cautious in their recording, 'even to the extent of workers not keeping any records when service users refused permission to do this' (SSI 1994b, para. 13.10). The intention here would be to try to protect people from the perceived stigma of HIV/AIDS, and some records were even written up in an 'idiosyncratic pattern of secrecy which rendered [them] meaningless' (para. 13.14). Again, confidentiality here has arguably veered over into secrecy, which does not serve the interests of service users or carers.

Confidentiality remains a problematic concept in social services practice. Can it ever be guaranteed as an absolute, and what do you do if you have given a guarantee and then feel you must break it? Can a confidence be breached when it has taken place in an overtly therapeutic interview? Some critics have complained that, in their experience: 'many social workers are extremely confused about the issue of confidentiality' (FRG 1987).

Others have been even less kindly disposed to the idea of confidentiality. It has been dismissed as 'not a significant issue' (Hadley et al. 1987, p. 93), or as something that exists only in theory rather than in practice (Bayley et al. 1987, p. 29), or as nothing more than a 'professional fetish' (Simpkin 1989). Even the influential Seebohm Report believed confidentiality based on a one-to-one relationship was 'anachronistic', but did see social services agencies holding personal information securely (Seebohm Report 1968, paras 656–62). Teamwork and community-based work are seen as inevitably loosening up on confidentiality: 'Confidentiality in a locally based setting cannot be a refuge to hide behind' (Bayley 1989).

Presumably, those who believe this still retain some concept of a line of confidentiality. I have sat through lurid tales of wife-swapping, re-told by social workers with all the salacious details, when the subject of discussion ostensibly was the admission of a 2-year-old to a day nursery. There might have been a 'need to know', but the case was never made. I have also heard people in child protection conferences say: 'I don't want this minuted but …' Why introduce it if you do not want it minuted? Anybody reading this who has worked in a social services department will be able to produce their own examples, and decide for themselves if confidentiality is an unnecessary, 'high-minded' principle.

Suggestions have been made that social workers and all employees in social services should be properly recognised as being part of a regulated profession, complete with a general council having oversight of standards of all kinds in the work (Parker 1990). At present no such council exists, but pressures from Europe to give social services employees equivalence with their colleagues in the European Union have kept up the argument that the UK should have some kind of general social services council. Such a council would hold a register of all practitioners, implement various sanctions against those offering poor practice, and would ultimately have the power to remove someone from the register. In investigating breaches of professional conduct, such a council would surely find itself pronouncing on issues of confidentiality (General Social Services Action Group 1992).

In the absence of such a council, practitioners may voluntarily join appropriate professional associations. The British Association of Social Workers has a membership that fluctuates between 8,000 and 10,000, which is estimated to be only 20 per cent of those practitioners who are eligible to join. However, the BASW probably has an influence wider than its immediate membership, and one of its earliest publications was a discussion paper on confidentiality (BASW 1971). Today its Code of Ethics places an obligation on all its members to treat personal information entrusted to them in confidence, and requires members to:

> respect the privacy of clients and others with whom they come into contact and confidential information gained in their relationship with them. (BASW 1986, para. 10(xi))

The BASW Code of Ethics also accepts that this obligation of confidence is not absolute, and that there will be times when it will be necessary to disclose information to others. In these circumstances, social workers:

> will divulge such information only with the consent of the client (or informant) except where there is clear evidence of serious danger to the client, worker, other persons or the community or in other circumstances judged exceptional, on the basis of professional consideration and consultation. (BASW 1986, para. 10(xi))

The Social Care Association (SCA) also represents employees in social services, and its 1988 AGM accepted a Code of Practice to guide its members. Personal information is to be kept confidential unless disclosure is in the client's interests, 'or where there is an overriding concern for the rights of other people' (SCA 1988, paras 4.1–4.4).

Both the BASW and the SCA accept that confidentiality may be broken where there is a demonstrable 'need to know'.

The 'need to know'

Implicit in the idea of confidentiality being protected by professional judgement is the idea that it will on occasions be necessary to disclose information to make it 'public'. Such thinking lies behind the common law and other administrative attempts to regulate the flow of personal information (see next section). A judgement has to be made that the third party has a 'need to know' certain personal information.

Although we have referred to disclosing information to make it 'public', we are, of course, referring to a public domain made up of other professionals and practitioners who make up the 'welfare network', rather than the public at large. Social services activities are carried out in an inter-disciplinary world, working alongside doctors, psychologists, nurses, education welfare officers, housing officials, social security officials, police officers, teachers and any other practitioners who might become involved in providing personal social services. It is this particular public domain that might have a 'need to know' personal information held by social services, and in turn may hold personal information that social services staff may 'need to know' to do their job. We have already noted in Chapter 3 a seemingly increasing 'need to know' being imposed on social services by the growth in the number of agencies requiring social workers to pass out information.

The concept of the 'need to know' is a familiar one, but one which is often reduced to cliché status. It effectively requires one professional to make an assessment of the work of another professional, and to make a decision as to how much information about a person they need in order to carry out their particular role.

In practice, it is contended that there is often little clarity about another practitioner's work and little thought put into the 'need to know' decision. There may well be a surfeit of information disclosed on the basis that 'you never know', rather than you 'need to know' – information passed on on the basis that it might possibly come in useful at some future point. At worst, this provides a surfeit of information, disclosed as a form of 'covering oneself', and if anything goes wrong, others can never say they didn't know!

Inter-disciplinary work and multi-disciplinary teamwork, along with the exchange of personal information, have long been promoted as desirable ways of providing personal social services: 'Everyone would lend it support in much the same way everyone would vote for a sunny summer' (CCETSW 1989, p. 8). This is seen as a more positive way of making full assessments and delivering services in work as varied as child protection and provision of community care services to older people. The desire to get the 'full picture' of what is happening in a family, for example, puts added pressure on the 'need to know' principle, in case you do not realise you have the missing jigsaw piece that everyone is looking for.

It might almost be said that information is sometimes exchanged indiscriminately rather than with any assessment of the 'need to know', because getting the 'full picture' is almost an end in itself, rather than the precursor to different courses of action by different professionals and practitioners. In child protection work in particular, social workers have been found taking 'a flexible line', rather than a 'strict interpretation of preserving client confidentiality, which makes child abuse investigations highly problematic' (Corby 1987, p. 51). Others have found that, even when confidentiality is specifically raised, it: 'did not reveal such widespread concern as might have been predicted from … statements to be found in the pages of professional journals ... considerations of confidentiality did not, in practice, inhibit the sharing of information at conferences' (Hallett and Stevenson 1980, p. 100), and indeed that: 'confidentiality ... is another potential block to effective cooperation, though one that seems to be more a block in theory than in practice.' (Bayley et al. 1987, p. 29).

Through the 1990s, pressure has built up to ensure that inter-disciplinary work increases its potential. In child protection work we now have much closer working arrangements between police and social workers, and in community care work between health and social services staff. Personal information may be exchanged on the understanding that the recipient has an obligation of confidence in handling it, but the fact that more and more information is being exchanged is not at issue.

Inter-disciplinary work is not always easy, and with practitioners coming from different educational and organisational backgrounds, with different ideas of status and aims and objectives, the potential for friction is ever present. It may even be that the exchange of personal information becomes the means of oiling the inter-disciplinary wheels to keep them moving, and has in turn become the lingua franca between different agencies and professional groups.

Sharing personal information may be done with the best of intentions to provide better services. The North Americans have coined the phrase 'need to nose' to suggest that the 'need to know' is being displaced, but that implies a deliberate, malicious intent which may not be present.

The exchange of too much personal information eventually may even lead to inaction, rather than action based on the 'need to know' principle. Practitioners are unable to sort out what is important from what is not important, and even suffer from 'anxiety overload' (Gurrey 1990).

Although we are now considering circumstances in which confidentiality may be broken, it is worth repeating that confidentiality remains an important base line. Just because it can be broken does not in any way undermine its importance. The idea of the 'need to know' underpins professional regulation, and also regulation by administrative and legal means.

Administrative regulations

Earlier, we described the practitioner in social services as being 'wrapped around' with administrative requirements imposed by the bureaucracy that employs him or her. That bureaucracy will, in turn, have its activities circumscribed by guidance from higher sources, including, in particular, the Department of Health.

Policies and procedures

Individual social services agencies, whether as departments of local authorities or as voluntary or private agencies, will develop their own policies and procedures, which will invariably include guidance on the conduct of staff handling personal information.

The Department of Health has issued Circular LAC(88)17 to all local authority directors of social services, requiring each department to draw up confidentiality policies and procedures, and recommending that departments devise a 'confidentiality statement', outlining policy, and invite all staff to sign it (DoH 1988, Part III). It is not clear how many social services departments have followed this circular to the letter, but many will have had good models of practice in place even before it was issued. (Circular LAC(88)17 formally expired on 1 January 1994, but has had its life extended indefinitely – see Local Authority Social Services letter LASSL(92)9, November 1992.) The circular could be applied equally to the independent and voluntary sector as well as the statutory. A separate circular covers Scotland (Scottish Education Department 1989a).

The publication of Circular LAC(88)17 followed an earlier draft version in 1986. In a covering letter the then DHSS said:

> The need to do this has arisen as a result of the growing interest in this subject arising from the data protection legislation and other developments. (DHSS 1986)

Those 'other developments' may have included the passing of the Police and Criminal Evidence Act 1984, and its designation of social work records as 'excluded' material (see pages 77–8), or possibly the debate on the mandatory reporting of child abuse to the police: something adjudged as *not* necessary (DHSS 1985, paras 12.3–12.4).

Whatever the reasons, Circular LAC(88)17 is the most definitive account we have from the Department of Health concerning guidance on confidentiality in the personal social services. It covers not just written records but also video and audio records and computer files. Its starting point is that:

> *all* personal information must be treated as confidential. Mutual trust between a social services department and those using its services, or involved in their care, is central to the successful provision of services both to the individual client and to clients in general. (DoH 1988, para. 15)

Information held on computer should be secure against unauthorised access, and the screens of video display units located so that unauthorised people cannot see them. Manual filing systems should be in secure metal cabinets, and one person in social services management made responsible for the security of all records in the department (paras 52–4).

Personal information should only be disclosed to those outside the social services department *with the consent* of the person to whom it applies, and to people who will further respect that it is confidential and who have a reasonable 'need to know' the information.

Having set this high standard of confidentiality, Circular LAC(88)17 then goes on to give examples of where the person's consent to disclose may *not* be necessary. Personal information, it is suggested, may be disclosed for 'social work purposes' to others in the department, including managers and other social carers, as well as to other parts of the local authority, such as the finance or legal department. Any co-operation with the NHS may take place without the person's consent, as may co-operation with committees of inquiry or the Social Services Inspectorate. Collaboration in the interests of child protection does not necessarily require consent, although, as in all these examples, good practice might dictate that it be obtained.

Consent may also not be necessary if disclosure is for 'exceptional' purposes. The Department of Health defines these as situations where legislation requires disclosure, such as a court wanting to see information relevant to matters within its jurisdiction, where disclosure might be in the interests of public health, an individual's health or the interests of the subject – for example, an abandoned baby, where the parents are being sought.

Disclosure to the police might also 'exceptionally be justified' to help them 'prevent, detect or prosecute a serious crime' (DoH 1988, para. 28). The request for information must come from an officer of at least superintendent rank, and satisfactory undertakings received that the information 'will be destroyed if the person is not prosecuted, or is discharged or acquitted' (*ibid.*). If a person is in physical danger, including a child, social services staff should make their own approaches to the police and not wait for a request for information (para. 30).

This advice leaves a number of outstanding questions – the problem of defining 'serious' crime, for example – although Circular LAC(88)17 suggests it should include crimes which have caused, or may cause, death, substantial financial gain, serious injury or serious harm to public order (DoH 1988, para. 29). At the end of the day, 'serious crime' may be a notoriously subjective concept.

The question of police requests only coming from superintendents again suggests a departure from the reality of every-day social work, when requests are more likely to come from more junior ranks. Exactly how social services staff can obtain 'satisfactory undertakings' that personal information will be destroyed by the police in certain circumstances remains a mystery.

Social workers are under no specific legal obligation to notify the police of crimes committed, and are only guided by the Department of Health and the general sense of civic duty that all citizens have 'to help police officers to prevent crime and discover offenders' (Home Office 1991a, Code C, para. 1A). When a London social worker was threatened by the Metropolitan Police with prosecution if he did not give them certain names, they were presumably going to use the common law to charge him ('Prosecution threat over client's letters', *Community Care*, 28 April 1983, p. 2). Conversely, when a member of staff at a voluntary social services agency in Worcestershire was murdered, police were given access to all the personal files to help them look for the offender; they undertook only to use this information for the murder inquiry ('Files seized after death', *Social Work Today*, 12 October 1989).

Apart from these basic principles that all information is confidential and should only be disclosed with consent except for social work or exceptional purposes, Circular LAC(88)17 advises all departments to draw up a confidentiality document that all staff would sign to agree that they understood the principles (DoH 1988, para. 39) and to work towards a duty of confidentiality being reflected in the terms and conditions of employment of staff. Ultimately, this would mean staff being:

> aware of their responsibilities towards subjects and donors and of the possibilities of disciplinary sanctions, including dismissal, where justified, for unauthorised disclosure of information. (para. 48)

Just how consistently social services departments have implemented this Department of Health guidance remains unclear.

One final point should be noted before we leave Circular LAC(88)17 and that is the emphasis placed on information passing to social services from health professionals. In the draft version of the circular issued in October 1986 there is no suggestion at all that personal information from health professionals should be treated any differently from any other personal information (DHSS 1986). The medical profession has always taken confidentiality seriously, and at least one public pronouncement from a doctor at the time declared that social workers, having no central registering body, should not have equal access to personal health information to health professionals (Dawson 1983, p. 55; see also Harbridge 1983).

Whether there was intense lobbying or not in the mid-1980s, the 1988 version of the circular requires social services staff receiving information from health professionals only to use the information for the purpose it was disclosed, not to pass it to others for whom it is not essential, and not to do so without the agreement of the health professionals. Failure to comply could lead to refusal to pass on further information (DoH 1988, paras 10–12).

In the mid-1990s the BMA, the Royal College of Nursing, the Health Visitors Association and other groups representing health professionals produced a draft bill to try to tighten up on confidentiality, and what they described as 'information creep' (Hall 1994; BMA et al. 1994). The annual report of the General Medical Council that year, which was published at almost the same time, revealed that over 100 complaints had been made against doctors for alleged breaches of confidentiality (GMC 1994, p. 16). The Department of Health in turn issued a draft circular somewhat akin to Circular LAC(88)17 to try to tighten up on confidentiality (DoH 1994c).

Local authority social services departments with procedures on confidentiality will probably have based them on Circular LAC(88)17, and overt breaches of confidentiality will no doubt result in disciplinary procedures for the offender. Managers will be expected to implement confidentiality procedures, but as with case recording itself, they might expect it to be an intrinsic part of the professionalism of a social worker (see Cockburn 1990, p. 56–7).

Complaints and representation

Throughout the 1980s a burgeoning users' rights movement was ever critical of the performance of the personal social services and demanded rights of redress. Some of these demands explicitly concerned access to personal information held by social services, and were acceded to in the Access to Personal Files Act 1987. Other demands were for a more open and less directive form of service that allowed for partnership and direct means of complaint if necessary.

For example, the advocacy movement during this period sought to have representatives of vulnerable people deal with the social services to improve the levels of service being offered. The idea was to give the users of services some added strength in arguing their case against the professionals. The Disabled Persons (Consultation, Representation and Services) Act 1986 gave statutory recognition to the advocacy movement, and Section 2 of the Act gave 'authorised representatives' the right to attend meetings and interviews and receive relevant documents and information. Unfortunately for those who had lobbied for this access, all those sections of the Act concerning advocates were quietly disposed of by the government, and although they remained on the statute book, they never became law (see Sutton 1991).

One of the government's arguments for dropping critical sections of the Act was that the new NHS and Community Care Act 1990 made them redundant. The NHS and Community Care Act (Section 50) and, running parallel to it, the Children Act 1989 (Section 26) both placed a legal requirement on local authorities to devise complaints and representation systems that would demonstrate a greater sense of commitment to service users. These new systems would enable complaints about service delivery to be taken up, and would include another avenue for redress for improper disclosure of personal information. Whether or not the NHS and Community Care Act offered a reasonable substitute for the unimplemented sections of the Disabled Persons Act remained debatable.

Complaints can be made directly to agency managers and directors, and in the case of local authorities, to locally elected councillors. They can also be fed into the new 'official' complaints procedures.

Once in place for adults (April 1991) and children (October 1991), complaints procedures had similar aims:

- to be an effective means of complaining;
- to ensure complaints were acted upon;
- to ensure a swift resolution;
- to allow those denied a service to have a means of redress;
- to allow independent review of complaints;
- to help managers and councillors to monitor the performance of social services.

Although it has been pointed out that the traditional nature of confidentiality in social work could militate against the openness required in a good complaints system (Dourado 1991), the new procedures could become a repository of complaints about breaches of confidentiality and inappropriate disclosures of personal information.

Complaints may also be made to the Commissioner for Local Administration (more popularly known as the Ombudsman or Ombudsperson). The commissioner can make findings of 'maladministration' and recommend payment of compensation by local authorities where that 'maladministration' has resulted in injustice. Two cases from the North of England demonstrate the commissioner's investigation of social services departments which were thought to have allowed the inappropriate disclosure of personal information.

In Leeds a social worker with the social services department was criticised by the commissioner's office for disclosing personal information to a senior advice worker in an unemployment advice centre. The advice worker was assisting with social security advice for a family with four children which the social worker was also helping. Liaison between the social worker and the advice worker took place, and the latter was advised when the two older children were admitted to care. The commissioner found maladministration to have taken place because the social worker also disclosed the reasons why the children had gone into care, which it was deemed the advice worker had no need to know (Commission for Local Administration in England 1988, Complaint No. 87/C/0123).

A more complex incident involving social workers from Barnsley Social Services Department took place in 1987. The social worker visited a family with children on the Child Protection Register and experienced some hostility from the family. Such hostility is not altogether unfamiliar to social workers, but on this occasion the father of the children was a nurse tutor for the local health authority and allegedly threatened to use his position to warn student nurses about how social services behaved in family situations such as his. The social worker released this information to his senior officers and a doctor from the health authority.

The social worker's actions in speaking as he did were *not* considered an improper disclosure by the commission. A formal approach taken by the senior social services officers to the health authority without visiting the complainant *was* thought improper, and constituted maladministration, if not an injustice (Commission for Local Administration in England 1989, Complaint No. 88/C/0331).

At a national level, complaints may also be made to the Data Protection Registrar, who will investigate inappropriate disclosures and other improprieties concerned with computer-held information. The Registrar is also planning in future to have oversight of non-computerised manual files as proposed by the 1994 Government Code of Practice on Access to Government Information (see page 74).

At present the registrar is empowered to follow up any alleged contravention of the Data Protection Act and has a duty to follow up complaints that raise 'a matter of substance' (Data Protection Act 1984, Section 36(2)). A section of the registrar's annual report is set aside for 'Complaints from Individuals', and lists a selection of the sort of complaints being made. The 1990 report, for example, contained a complaint from a woman concerned over references to her 'mental condition' on a local authority computer print-out. The council refused to change them when she asked for amendments, but did so when the registrar took up her complaint (DPR 1990, p. 11). In the year to 31 March 1994 the registrar dealt with 2,889 complaints about computer use in all sectors of society (DPR 1994, p. 34).

Complaints and complaints mechanisms have become an important adjunct to administrative bureaucracies in the 1990s, whether in the public, voluntary or private sectors. The ethos has been taken up in the central government idea of charters, and in particular the Citizen's Charter, designed to raise quality standards in public life and 'make public services answer better to the wishes of their users' (Citizen's Charter 1991, p. 2). The direct impact of the Citizen's Charter on the personal social services has not been spelt out in detail, but the appointment of local lay assessors and adjudicators has been suggested (Citizen's Charter 1991, p. 43).

Guidance, codes of practice and circulars

The Department of Health, in keeping with other offices of State, publishes regular bulletins of guidance to local authorities on how they should conduct their activities. This guidance will be in the form of circulars, codes of practice or simply as volumes of guidance. The Children Act 1989, for example, led to nine volumes of guidance. The status of such guidance can be problematic as it does not formally constitute law, even though it is taken seriously by local authorities and others, and its effect in practice may not be dissimilar to a legal enactment. Some have termed it 'quasi-legislation' (Ganz 1987), and others made reference to a 'trend to coded practice' (Baldwin 1988).

The Local Authority Social Services Act 1970, Section 7, states that: 'local authorities shall in the exercise of their social services functions … act under the general guidance of the Secretary of State'. Such a wording seems to imply that it is mandatory for social services departments to follow guidance. Section 7 was reinforced by the NHS and Community Care Act 1990, Section 50, which introduced a new Section 7A into the Local Authority Social Services Act as a prelude to the enormous amount of guidance on community care that was duly delivered.

Counsel's opinion has been sought in the past on the status of Section 7, and such opinion felt that it did mean guidance had to be followed, and it was therefore 'mandatory' to do so. The government confirmed that that was the position as they understood it (Commission for Local Administration in England 1986, Complaint No. 956/Y/84). Section 7 remains untested in the courts, unlike the Housing Act 1985, Section 71, which requires local authorities to have regard to the Department of Environment's Code of Guidance on Homelessness. The courts have ruled that the code, first issued under the earlier Housing (Homeless Persons) Act 1977, Section 12, should not be regarded as a binding statute (*De Falcro, Silvestri* v. *Crawley Borough Council* [1980] QB 460 CA).

When the London Borough of Sutton cited Department of Health guidance that required them to only approve childminders who would not use corporal punishment on children left in their charge, it was suggested to them that the law differed from guidance. Although there was a requirement to abide by guidance under Section 7 of the Local Authority Social Services Act, the guidance should not have been elevated into a blanket policy, and anyway it encouraged partnership with parents, and in this case the parent had given the childminder permission to smack the child (*Sutton Borough Council* v. *Davis, The Times* Law Report, 17 March 1994).

So the status of Section 7 remains somewhat enigmatic (for a fuller discussion see DoH 1989b, pp. 2–3). What we can say is that circulars and guidance are none the less issued regularly to directors of social services, and they are taken seriously and acted upon. Many of them contain references to confidentiality and the need to maintain records and process personal information appropriately. Sometimes, as we saw with Circular LAC(88)17, confidentiality may be the sole topic of a circular.

Social services may have to take note of circulars and guidance issued by government departments other than the Department of Health, if there are implications for social services. Sometimes guidance is issued jointly by more than one department, such as the important document, *Working Together*, issued jointly by the Home Office, Department of Health, Department of Education and Science and the Welsh Office (Home Office et al. 1991). The same four departments also issued the circular on disclosure of police-held criminal convictions for child care 'checks' (Home Office et al. 1993).

Another form of guidance arrives on the desk of social services directors from the offices of the Department of Health's Social Services Inspectorate (SSI). Although not always formal guidance as such, the SSI produces reports on various subjects or on services it has looked at, and these reports invariably contain recommendations which all directors take note of. If the report concerns a service which is the responsibility of a particular director, the expectation is that recommendations will be followed and the SSI will retain a monitoring brief.

The Data Protection Registrar offers guidance on computer-held information and publishes regular guidance notes. The registrar also has a duty under the Data Protection Act to encourage the development of codes of practice amongst computer users:

> to encourage trade associations or other bodies representing data users to prepare, and to disseminate to their members, codes of practice for guidance in complying with the data protection principles. (Data Protection Act 1984, Section 36(4))

Although there is a legal duty on the registrar, the resulting codes are purely voluntary arrangements to assist individuals in exercising their rights and computer users in meeting their obligations. The registrar is willing to help computer users draw up codes, and will comment on drafts; he or she will also take such codes into account in the event of a complaint, although this will not necessarily protect the user from legal action (see also DPR 1985 and 1986a). In the Republic of Ireland a code of practice drawn up under their data protection legislation does take on the force of law (Data Protection Act 1988, Section 13(1)).

Social services agencies have been slower than most to take on the new information technology to assist their work, but none the less, as we have already seen, did devise an early code of practice. The Ethics and Security Sub-Group of the Local Authorities Management Service and Computer

Applications Group (LAMSAC) produced its own draft code of practice for social services departments (see Pearce et al. 1988, pp. 56–79).

At central government level, moves have been made towards more open government that have brought new safeguards on personal information in their wake. A White Paper in 1993 (Chancellor of the Duchy of Lancaster 1993) was followed by a Code of Practice on Access to Government Information in April 1994. The government sought to make general information more publicly accessible in its departments, the NHS, local authorities, the police, schools and universities. In so doing it had to guard against:

> Unwarranted disclosure to a third party of personal information about any person (including a deceased person) or any other disclosure which would constitute or could facilitate an unwarranted invasion of privacy. (Citizen's Charter 1994, p. 8)

In attempting to balance this move towards more freedom of information against a need to protect personal information disclosure, the government also made another new departure. Personal information on manual files was to be opened up to the subjects of those files along similar lines to that held on computers (Chancellor of the Duchy of Lancaster 1993, para. 5.12). The Data Protection Registrar, who had oversight of computer data, was to take on the enforcement of a right of subject access to these manually-held government files.

Legal regulation

If professional and administrative regulation has not been able to police the circulation of personal information effectively, legal regulation can be considered as a fall-back position, offering yet another means of regulation, and at times giving people a formal means of redress if they think their confidences have been abused. Both the common law and statutory law play a part in this regulation.

Common law

The common law of the UK has been described as the accumulated wisdom of the country as expressed through judicial proceedings. At its best, the common law is seen as flexible and dynamic in expressing the law within the spirit of the times and in a manner that is not hidebound by the statutory 'letter of the law'.

In terms of personal information and privacy, the common law places an obligation of confidence around any information passed between people in a contractual relationship, a relationship between employers and employees, and between bankers and professional advisers and their clients. Amongst professional advisers, we might include social workers and other social services personnel.

The expectation is that information – personal or otherwise – exchanged in given circumstances becomes 'impressed' with an obligation of confidence. Failure to maintain that confidence, either deliberately or negligently, could lead to a civil action in the High Court for 'breach of confidence'. The court can issue injunctions to prevent disclosure, or award damages to compensate a plaintiff for any harm caused.

In practice, 'breach of confidence' actions have hardly, if ever, been used against social services staff, and the action is far more likely to be used when the disclosure has been of non-personal commercial information within the business world from which someone has made monetary gain. Having said that, there is no reason in law why a 'breach of confidence' action should not be taken against the simple disclosure of personal information by a social worker by someone who thinks they have acted inappropriately.

The Law Commission has summarised the action for breach of confidence as being:

> a civil remedy affording protection against the disclosure or use of information which is not publicly known and which has been entrusted to a person in circumstances imposing an obligation not to disclose or use that information without the authority of the person who imparted it. (Law Commission 1981, p. 10)

The common law does recognise that the right to confidentiality is not absolute and recognises a number of situations when it would still be permissible to disclose personal information. In turn, these situations become the defence against any action for breach of confidence, and include information revealing a past or future crime, a fraud or anything involving national security, and information that might indicate somebody or something was going to endanger the public in some way. In more general terms, a defence against an action for breach of confidence could also be mounted on the basis that the information was already in the public domain, or that there was a 'public interest' in it being in the public domain.

A full explanation of the intricacies of the law on breach of confidence is beyond the scope of this book, and the reader is referred to other sources (for example, Law Commission 1981; Gurry 1984; Wacks 1989, Chapter 3). We do, however, need to explore the exceptions to the common law presumption of confidentiality.

Disclosure ordered by a court   Courts of law can compel the disclosure of social services records if it will assist judicial proceedings. This has not always been the case, and at one time social services records enjoyed a much tighter definition of 'privilege', comparable almost to that of the 'legal privilege' between lawyer and client. Such 'public interest immunity' was considered particularly relevant to child care records.

In an early case, Lord Denning had ruled on social work records:

> On principle I hold that these case notes and records should not be disclosed at the instance of another party to the suit. There may be exceptional circumstances in which the court might overrule the privilege, but certainly not in this case. (*Re D (Infants)* [1970] 1 All ER 1088)

Public interest immunity was cited again as a reason for denying a woman information from the NSPCC when she wanted to know who had reported her (maliciously) to that agency. Disclosure would, it was argued, adversely affect social work relations with clients and deter others from making appropriate referrals (*D* v. *NSPCC* [1978] AC 171 HL(E)).

Since then, courts have moved slowly away from public interest immunity for social services records. In the light of greater openness generally in society and in the general public interest that the administration of justice requires the truth to come out, the strict protections of the past have been relaxed (*Re M (A Minor) (Disclosure of Material)* [1990] 2 FLR 36; see also Downey 1990). With open access policies allowing clients to see their files (see Chapter 5) social services should even consider voluntary disclosure (*R* v. *Hampshire CC ex parte K* [1990] 1 FLR 330). In other events the courts will decide after balancing the interests of confidentiality against the administration of justice (Langdale and Maskrey 1994).

Disclosure can be ordered in civil and criminal cases. In the latter it is most frequently encountered when prosecution of an alleged perpetrator of abuse against a child is coming to court. Social workers may fear for the welfare of the child or damage to their relationship with the child if confidential records are made available to defence lawyers to be later cited in the public forum of the court (Gilham 1994; see also *Re K (Family Division), The Independent*, Law Report, 23 November 1993).

One unintended consequence of disclosing relevant evidence to the defence before a trial gets under way has been the misuse of witness statements in sexual offences cases. Statements, some of which had been made by children, were noted to be circulating as a form of pornography in their own right ('Rape statements "used as porn"', *Guardian*, 26 October 1989). Video recordings of children's evidence were similarly believed to be getting into the wrong hands through the disclosure procedures (Handscomb 1991).

The Home Office acknowledged the problem in a consultation paper and believed that solicitors had a role to play in ensuring the proper use of witness statements, but also floated the idea of giving access but not possession of statements to defendants (Home Office 1991b). The Home Office/DHSS guidance on video-taping children's evidence advised that defendants not represented by a solicitor should have access to such evidence only 'under strict police supervision' or borrow it only after giving a written undertaking about the protection he or she would provide regarding the tape (Home Office/DoH 1992, para. 4.12).

In the course of a criminal investigation, the courts may also order social services departments and any other social work agency to hand over records and material to the police. The Department of Health advises that cooperation should normally be forthcoming without recourse to the courts, especially if a serious crime is under investigation. Indeed, as we have seen, social services should not even wait to be asked by the police if they have such information (DoH 1988, para. 30).

If social services should decide *not* to disclose information to the police, they would be entitled to cite their general obligation of confidence and the provisions of the Police and Criminal Evidence Act 1984, which designates social work records as 'excluded material' (Sections 11–12). 'Excluded material' also includes medical and journalistic records, which – along with 'special procedure material' (Section 14), including information such as bank accounts – can be legitimately withheld from the police. Magistrates cannot issue a warrant to search for 'excluded' or 'special procedure' material.

This protection of social services records from police seizure was rigorously campaigned for as the Police and Criminal Evidence Bill went through parliament. Even the normally temperate British Association of Social Workers was moved to say that, if records were not 'excluded', 'social workers may have to defy [the law] on occasions' (BASW 1983, p. 41; see also 'Fight to keep client records from police and tax men', *Community Care*, 26 April 1984, p. 5).

If the police are determined to see social services records which are being denied them, they can raise the stakes and seek legal support at a higher level. The police can apply to a circuit judge for a Production Order, requiring social services to hand over documentation whether or not it is designated as 'excluded material'. An officer of at least superintendent level must make the decision to apply (Home Office 1991a, Code B, para. 2.4). The police must believe it will help solve a serious crime, may contain relevant evidence and be of substantial value. They must also have tried other ways of obtaining it and believe it is in the public interest to obtain it (PACE 1984, Section 9 and Schedule 1). A Production Order will be granted if a search for the material could have been authorised by any laws prior to PACE.

The main difference in applying for a Production Order rather than a magistrate's search warrant is that notice must be given to the person or organisation holding the information, and they can give their reasons for opposing the application in court. The procedure is inter-partes, rather than ex-parte where the other person may not necessarily even be aware of the application. An ex-parte application for a search warrant rather than a Production Order can be made for 'excluded material' if the police can demonstrate why this is the best way of proceeding (PACE 1984, Schedule 1, paras 12–15). In practice it has been pointed out that ex-parte applications in these circumstances are rare because the holders of personal information are not usually the *subjects* of that information. Indeed, the subject may be totally unaware of the application for a Production Order:

> The practical effect of these decisions is that the person most affected by the order and with an interest in resisting the police's application is given no opportunity whatever to challenge the application. (Zuckerman 1990)

It is left to the circuit judge to balance the individual's entitlement to confidentiality against the public interest of crime control.

Once a Production Order or search warrant has been granted, the search should be under the charge of an officer of the rank of inspector or above. Requests for documents are made to 'a person in authority and with responsibility for the documents' (Home Office 1991a, Code B, para. 5B) and, if necessary, the police can inspect the index to files and 'inspect any file which, according to the index, appears to contain any of the material sought' (para. 5.14).

Production Orders have been granted in relation to medical information which has duly been handed to the police (although later successfully challenged in the courts – *R* v. *Central Criminal Court ex parte Brown*, *The Times* Law Report, 7 September 1992). A Schedule 1 warrant was also refused when police wanted access to medical files to search for people with a certain blood group as part of a murder inquiry. The circuit judge decided that too many people's confidences would be breached in what amounted to a police 'trawl', and there was no guarantee it would be of value in the investigation (Schutte 1989).

No order is known to have been granted regarding information held by social services and in view of the close working arrangements now in place between police and social services, it seems unlikely that such an order will ever be made (see also Hewson 1993).

Statutory requirement to allow access   A person who has been appointed as a guardian ad litem under the Children Act has a right of access to local authority social services records maintained for the authority to apply for an order under the Act, or indeed maintained for any other purposes (Children Act 1989, Section 42, as amended by the Courts and Legal Services Act 1990, Schedule 16, para. 18(2)).

The Commissioner for Local Administration has a statutory right of access to social services records in order to carry out his or her investigations. Local authority officers (and members) must produce records for them as required (Local Government Act 1974, Sections 28–9).

Authorised inspectors of private children's homes and other services for children are entitled to see any records they need to (Children Act 1989, Section 80(4)), as are inspectors of private residential care establishments, whether for elderly people or any other age-group (Registered Homes Act 1984, Section 17(3)). Anybody appointed by the Secretary of State to hold an inquiry in relation to children's services would have a right of access to any relevant records (Children Act 1989, Section 81).

The government's decision to bring in lay inspectors as part of general inspection procedures has caused some problems when they receive personal information as part of their duties. The Social Services Inspectorate suggests:

> all lay assessors should ... give a written undertaking to safeguard the confidentiality of information they receive in the course of their duties. (SSI 1994c, para. 2.24)

Where there is a right of subject access   This arises when the law has given a person the right to see what is held on them on formal files (see Chapter 5).

To assist someone performing a public or statutory duty   In her capacity as an elected member on a Birmingham Housing Committee, Councillor Willetts was given information about a person's rent arrears, together with the information that the person had a criminal record, was a foster-parent for the local authority and had applied to become an adoptive parent. Councillor Willetts asked to see the social work file on the family, and after due deliberation the Director of Social Services decided she could. At this point a community law centre acting for the prospective adoptors stepped in and sought a judicial review of the director's decision.

The judicial review became a test case and went through to the House of Lords, which finally held that the decision of the director was correct, and that the councillor was indeed entitled to see the file. The House of Lords's ruling was greeted with some dismay in social work circles, and the BASW called it 'an extremely dangerous precedent' (BASW 1983, p. 40). The Law Lords, however, were quite clear that:

> Each member of the Social Services Committee is entitled by virtue of his office to see all the papers which have come into the possession of a social worker in the course of his duties as an employee of the Council. There is no room for any secrecy as between a social worker and a member of the Social Services Committee. (*Birmingham District Council* v. *O* [1983] 1 All ER 497 HL)

Councillors not on the social services committee could have access to records if they needed it in order to carry out their public duties. No distinction was made in the case of documentation held by a worker, and no less than 'all the papers' should be handed over on legitimate request. This presumably includes any odd scraps of notes passed between workers or between a service user and a worker.

In a subsequent commentary on the ruling, Harris considered there to be three reasons why councillors might want access to files: first, in order to check the quality of the records themselves; second, to query matters that had been brought personally to their attention, and finally, in cases where special inquiries had been instituted, such as in the case of a child's or other service user's death. Harris did express concern that some maverick councillors could not be trusted to keep such information confidential (Harris 1984), even though all councillors are bound by a code of conduct which requires:

> never disclose or use confidential information for the personal advantage of yourself or of anyone known to you, or to the disadvantage or the discredit of the Council or anyone else. (DoE 1990, para. 26)

However, the principle remains established that personal information on a social services file should be disclosed if it will assist someone performing a public or statutory duty. A mere interest in seeing the information will not suffice, and a clear 'need to know' must be established. The principle was reaffirmed in the case of *R* v. *Hackney LBC ex parte Gamper* [1985] 3 All ER 275.

When Victoria Gillick claimed access to personal information held by a health authority about her daughter, she did so, she argued, in order to carry out her parental duties. The courts held that parental duties were not the same as public or statutory duties, and therefore did not agree that she had an automatic right of access to the information. A complicating factor was the age of the child and her capacity to consent to the treatment she had sought from the health authority. If she was competent to make decisions about treatment, it followed that she was entitled to the same confidentiality that all patients are entitled to (*Gillick* v. *West Norfolk and Wisbech Area Health Authority* [1985] 3 All ER 402; see also BMA et al. 1993).

Where it is in the public interest   Confidentiality may be breached in the case of matters of public interest, including a crime or something that might endanger the public. Even the normally sacrosanct legal privilege of confidentiality between a solicitor and his or her client might need to be breached if, say, a child was threatened with injury or abduction (White 1992), and between a doctor and patient, again if there was considered to be a danger to the public caused, say, by a person's mental health (*W* v. *Edgell* [1989] 1 All ER 1089 CA; *R* v. *Crozier*, *The Independent* Law Report, 11 May 1990).

For social services employees, the common law is now spelt out in Department of Health Circular LAC(88)17 (see pages 67–8), in the sections covering 'exceptional purposes'. These include matters of public health, serious crime and anything else deemed in the 'public interest'. Following the case of *W*. v. *Edgell*, it would seem proper for social services to disclose personal information about a person considered 'dangerous' and where there was felt to be a need to protect the public.

Statutory law

A number of statutory law enactments offer safeguards to prevent the indiscriminate circulation of personal information. Those of particular relevance to social services are dealt with below.

The Rehabilitation of Offenders Act 1974   At first sight, the Rehabilitation of Offenders Act 1974 would not appear to bear directly on the actions of social services agencies. The Act allows certain offenders who have not re-offended after given periods of time to regard their convictions as 'spent'. If asked about them, they are not legally obliged to disclose their existence, and anyone else with official access to those records commits an offence if he or she discloses a record that could legitimately be considered 'spent'.

The relevance of this to local authority social services departments is apparent when we consider that they are in receipt of criminal records from the police on an almost daily basis. Nationally, the police made around 665,000 disclosures to local authorities in the year ending 31 March 1993 (Home Office 1993a, para. 23). These disclosures are intended to screen out those considered a risk to children as employees, foster-parents, childminders and adoptive parents. Evidence of convictions that might put children at risk is sought, and 'exemptions' to the Rehabilitation of Offenders Act apply to this exercise, in which case *no* convictions are considered 'spent'.

As this personal information on criminal records is considered particularly sensitive, local authority staff must ensure the information is only released within a department to those who need to see it, kept securely until a judgement is made, and afterwards it must be destroyed (unless used for adoption and fostering cases) (Home Office et al. 1993, paras 19 and 33). Information leaking out of an authority could otherwise constitute an offence under the Rehabilitation of Offenders Act 1974, Section 9. 'Official records' of criminal convictions are defined in the Act as not just records held by the police and courts, but also local government records (Section 9(1)).

The Data Protection Act 1984   The growing concerns in Western societies over the use of computers to process personal information were traced in Chapter 1. The Organisation for Economic Co-operation and Development (OECD) and the Council of Europe produced guidelines and a convention on how the individual citizen might be protected from unnecessary loss of information privacy in the face of the all-pervading computer (OECD 1980; Council of Europe 1980).

In the UK, the Lindop Committee had already explored aspects of the 'computer problem' (Lindop Report 1978), and based on the findings of the committee and the international declarations, the government produced a White Paper proposing data protection legislation in 1982 (Home Office 1982). The Home Office spoke eloquently of the UK having a 'key role at a crossroads on the international data highway' (para. 25). Others were less enthusiastic.

There was a widespread feeling that the White Paper had done only the minimum necessary to enable the UK to ratify the Council of Europe convention, and that the focus was on enabling UK industry to continue to operate freely in the international markets rather than any concern for protecting individuals. The chair of the Lindop Committee described the White Paper as 'rather scanty' (Lindop 1983, p. 25), and from a social work perspective, the BASW wanted a strengthening of the Data Protection Office so that it was 'seen as strong and credible' (BASW 1982, p. 8).

The Data Protection Act 1984 which duly emerged and allowed the UK to ratify the Council of Europe convention was directed more towards industry and commerce than it was toward public bureaucracies (see, for example, Dolan 1986). Part of the underlying thinking behind the OECD guidelines and Council of Europe convention was the need for harmonisation between countries in the interests of international trade that required uninterrupted cross-border flows of data.

The Data Protection Act applies to all personal information held on computers, unless kept for personal use at home or given other exemptions. The owners of the computers, known in the Act as 'data users', must register their use and let it be known what sort of data they hold, why they hold it, the sources it comes from and who they might disclose it to, nationally and internationally. Failure to register is an offence.

Underpinning the Data Protection Act were the eight data protection principles set down by the Council of Europe convention. The principles were reproduced in Schedule 1 of the Act, together with a commentary on how they should be interpreted:

1   Information making up personal data should be obtained and processed fairly and lawfully.
2   Personal data should be held only for specified and lawful purposes.

3 Personal data held for one purpose should not be used or disclosed in any manner incompatible with that purpose.
4 Personal data held should be adequate, relevant and not excessive in relation to that purpose.
5 Personal data should be accurate and, where necessary, kept up to date.
6 Personal data should not be kept for longer than is necessary for its purpose.
7 An individual shall be entitled

 a at reasonable intervals and without undue delay or expense
  i to be informed by any Data User whether he holds personal data of which the individual is the subject, and
  ii to access to any such data, and
 b where appropriate, to have such data corrected or erased.

8 Security measures should be taken against unauthorised access to personal data, or alteration, disclosure or destruction of it.

The social services community could have no quarrel with any of these principles, which accorded with the professional understanding of confidentiality in social work and the emerging administrative regulation that existed. There could be no quarrel either, because in 1984 very few social services departments used information technology to process data. In due course, some regulations did appear that were specifically aimed at social services, and covered arrangements to give subject access to computer-held information (see Chapter 5).

The Data Protection Act 1984 created the office of Data Protection Registrar to oversee implementation of the Act. The registrar may serve notices on people to enforce compliance with the Act and its principles. These notices might specify action that must be taken, be it a de-registration notice cancelling all or part of a register entry or a transfer prohibition notice preventing transfer overseas.

Individuals whose personal details are stored on computer are termed 'data subjects'. Data subjects are given the right to see the information held on them – subject access – and can take legal action for unauthorised disclosure or the storing of inaccurate information (see Chapter 5). They may also make complaints to the registrar, who can follow them up, and if they are substantive, has a *duty* to follow them up.

As a new area of social policy, the newly-appointed registrar was inevitably feeling his way in the early days of the Act's implementation. Both the registrar and the public as 'users' and 'subjects' were on a learning curve (Raab 1993). An initial strategy was based on four measures:

1 to provide an effective complaints service to aggrieved data subjects;

2   to support codes of practice and other appropriate procedures and techniques developed by data users;
3   to institute the register of users;
4   to implement the Act as simply as possible for both 'user' and 'subject'.
    (DPR 1986b)

The registrar had to walk a tightrope between educating people (and himself) on the one hand and enforcing and regulating on the other. The first post-holder, Eric Howe, was under no illusions that 'the Act presents a massive educational challenge' (House of Commons 1990, Minutes of Evidence, p. 3). The dissemination of leaflets, guidance notes, an annual report and advertising was a central part of the registrar's job. A Data Protection Tribunal was formed to hear appeals from data users and data subjects and give rulings on points of law (Data Protection Tribunal Rules 1985, SI 1985 No. 1899).

Because they hold personal information on computers, social services are liable to the regulating influences of the Data Protection Act. The registrar, as we have seen, has to balance his or her role between that of 'bullish' enforcer, using all the sanctions available, and that of 'educator' and general promoter of the data protection principles as a new form of public policy (see, for example, Aldhouse 1991). In doing so, the registrar experienced exactly the same dilemmas as all other data protection registrars and commissioners, wherever they had come into being across the world (see, for example, Flaherty 1989; Bennett 1992).

Not everyone was happy about the registrar's performance, and critics have pointed out 'glaring holes' in the Data Protection Act. Up to 100,000 organisations were thought to be holding personal information on their computers illegally, many people knew nothing of their rights under the Act, and the registrar was criticised for not being tough enough in using his statutory powers ('"Glaring holes" in computer data Act', *The Independent*, 20 August 1993). Similar comments came from a senior member of staff when he left the Data Protection Registrar's office – including a lack of accountability, an obsession with privacy taken to unnecessary extremes, and a reaction to news stories rather than genuine complaints (Watts 1994).

In 1994 a private member's bill was published (see page 15) that would have replicated the central provisions of the 1984 Act and added on the requirements of the draft European Directive on Data Protection (reference COM (92)422 Final SYN 287). The registrar would have become the commissioner, the categories of sensitive data enlarged and the Act extended to cover manual files as well as computer-held information.

The Local Government (Access to Information) Act 1985   At times, personal information held by social services departments must be presented to committees of elected members for various decisions. The public may also be entitled to attend these meetings, and legal safeguards have been put in place to balance the public's right to know what is going on in local government with the need to regulate and prevent the disclosure of certain personal information applicable to identified individuals.

The Local Authorities (Admission of the Press to Meetings) Act 1908 opened up council meetings to the press, and the Public Bodies (Admission to Meetings) Act 1960 opened them up to the public. The Public Bodies Act was later amended to give the press and public new rights of access to committee meetings as well as full council meetings (Local Government Act 1972, Section 100). Inherent to this legislation was the ability for a council or committee to decide that the press and public be excluded from certain parts of a meeting if personal information of a confidential nature was being discussed.

The Local Government (Access to Information) Act 1985 extended our ideas of open government by permitting public access to committee and council documents and reports three days before meetings, and again after a meeting. The Local Government Act 1985 amended the Local Government Act 1972, again to ensure confidentiality of certain information on both a mandatory (Local Government Act 1972, Section 100A(3)) and discretionary basis (Section 100A(4)). Exempt information is listed in the amended Part 1 of Schedule 12A of the 1972 Act, and for social services purposes we should note that it includes reports on applicants for or recipients of any service provided by the authority, and information relating to the adoption, care, fostering or education of any particular child.

The ability to exclude the press and public from council and committee meetings when personal information is being discussed, and to exempt documents from public inspection for the same reason, should amount to a sufficient safeguard for the confidentiality of personal information held by social services. At the time of the introduction of the Local Government Act 1985 the then Secretary of the Association of Directors of Social Services felt it presented no critical problems about access to personal information ('Access to information: Councils happy with Act's safeguards', *Social Services Insight*, 5–12 April 1986), and no subsequent difficulties of any major import have come to light. At the time of writing, the Policy Studies Institute was conducting a review of the workings of the Act, on behalf of the Department of the Environment and the Association of Metropolitan Authorities.

The Computer Misuse Act 1990   The increased availability of personal computers that could network with other computer systems brought with it the possibility of anti-social computer-based activities. Prime amongst these are the 'hackers' who gain unauthorised access to computers and computer systems and those who release so-called 'viruses' into computer systems that effectively result in criminal damage to those systems.

The Computer Misuse Act 1990 stemmed from a private member's bill, and sought to create new offences around unauthorised access and 'modification', and to give the courts powers to deal with them. During debate on the bill, it was estimated that 'hacking' cost UK computer users some £400 million a year, and yet 'we find ourselves in the 1990's with a new well-defined mischief that the law does not address at all' (*Hansard*, 9 February 1990, Cols. 1,134–5). Effectively, the Computer Misuse Act is a statutory realisation of Principle 8 of the Data Protection Act principles.

The Human Fertilisation and Embryology Act 1990   Social workers and counsellors have a clearly defined role in respect of people seeking help from fertility treatment centres. The process of assisted reproduction, offered by the NHS or privately, is an anxious time for the people undergoing treatment, and there is a legal requirement for centres to employ social workers and counsellors (see King's Fund Centre 1991, Appendix 1). The Human Fertilisation and Embryology Act 1990 places a direct legal obligation on treatment centre staff to hold personal information in confidence (Sections 33(5)–33(7); see also HFEA 1993, Part 10).

Other legislation   All these Acts of parliament have had something to say on the circulation of personal information. Others that might have been mentioned but have less direct relevance for social workers include the Road Traffic Act 1988, Section 172, which requires any person, if so requested by the police, to give information which might lead to the identification of a person who has committed an offence under the Act, or the Prevention of Terrorism (Temporary Provisions) Act 1989, Section 18, which makes the withholding of information an offence when that information could lead to either the prevention of an offence or detection and prosecution of an offender.

Judicial review

The use of judicial review to examine the way in which a public body makes decisions involves an application to the High Court. The court will duly use its supervisory jurisdiction over a public body – including a local authority – and examine the decision-making process of that body. It should be noted that it is not the decision as such that is examined, but the process by which the decision has been reached. Judicial review has from time to time been used to look at local authority decision-making in relation to the circulation of personal information. Three examples can be cited.

The first we have already come across in Chapter 3 (see page 46) with reference to the nature of Child Protection Registers. Officers of Norfolk Social Services recorded personal information on an alleged child abuser at a child protection conference. Although the man had been interviewed by the police, no charge or prosecution resulted. None the less, the child protection conference felt concerned enough to put the child's name on the register and to tell the man's employers about the allegations made about him.

As a result, the man – a 55-year-old plumber of previous good character – was suspended from work while his employers looked into the allegations for themselves. The man was doubly aggrieved because the social services department staff had not told him they were going to notify his employers. He applied for a judicial review of the department's decision-making.

Norfolk Social Services argued in their defence that this was an 'internal administrative matter' that should not be subject to judicial review. The court thought otherwise and found in favour of the applicant. The social services department was described as having acted 'unfairly, unreasonably and in breach of natural justice'. The Child Protection Register was described as having 'dangerous potential as an instrument of injustice or oppression' (*R* v. *Norfolk CC ex parte M* [1989] 2 All ER 359).

Towards the end of 1990, another man sought a judicial review of the way in which Devon Social Services had given out personal information held on him. The man, referred to in the courts as 'Mr L' lived with a woman as man and wife and shared the home with her two children. Following accusations of interfering with the children, an examination by a paediatrician was followed by a child protection conference which placed the children's names on the Child Protection Register. Mr L was arrested and questioned by the police, but as in Norfolk, no criminal proceedings were ever instituted against him.

Mr L left the woman's home he had been living in and later moved in with another woman and her children. When this came to the notice of social services, they duly visited the man's new home to tell the woman what had happened previously. As a result, Mr L left the home, only to later move in with yet another woman with children in similar circumstances. Again social services became aware of the situation, and again they visited to tell the woman of the background as they saw it. Mr L again left, joined another household, and for a third time had another social work visit.

At this point, Mr L went to a solicitor to make complaints against the social services department and to ask if they would stop disseminating their beliefs about him to mothers of children he had chosen to live with. After an exchange of correspondence, an application was made for a judicial review of the way in which Devon County Council were reaching their decisions. The High Court eventually ruled that Devon had acted properly, and dismissed the application. The social workers had acted in good faith, had a statutory obligation to protect the welfare of the children, and even if Mr L had suffered a prejudice, his interests came second to those of the children (*R v. Devon CC ex parte L* [1991] 2 FLR 541).

Others have criticised the Devon case as being 'highly disturbing' and based on 'fallacious reasoning' (Hayes 1992). One reason for dismissing the application was that no decision had been made that was capable of review, because there had been no meeting and no written decision before the social workers had visited Mr L. It was as though the decisions belonged to the social workers and not the local authority. As Hayes writes, this is 'to confuse the form in which a decision is reached and the manner of its recording with the substance of whether a decision had been made' (*ibid.*). Hayes believes Devon County Council were in breach of Article 8 of the European Convention on Human Rights, which says people have a right to a private family life.

In London, a judicial review looked at a disclosure of personal information with some resemblance to the Devon case. A child in foster-care made allegations of sexual abuse against the foster-parents, and the placement was duly ended pending investigations. The child was removed to another foster-home and the circumstances explained to the new carers. As part of the explanation, staff of the social services department disclosed the name of the previous foster-carer.

As with the Norfolk and Devon cases, no proof was ever established that the first foster-parent had carried out any of the acts he was accused of. No charge or prosecution followed. The foster-parent objected to his name being given out, along with the allegations, and applied for a judicial review of the decision to do so.

The court held that social services had to balance the needs of the child against the consequences to any adults. It was felt that no such balancing had been carried out, and that a simple policy of full disclosure to the new foster-carers had taken place. The court held this to be the wrong way to make a decision of this nature and suggested that a withholding of the first carer's name would have been appropriate (*R v. Lewisham LBC ex parte P* [1991] 3 All ER 529).

The European dimension

We noted in Chapter 1 that data protection and privacy have often taken a higher profile at international level than at a domestic level of government. Although they may not have a direct impact on social services, we should briefly note here the various European and international forums that exist to circumscribe the outer rings of our diagram of regulation (see Figure 4.1).

The Council of Europe

The Council of Europe has historically been the most influential body over-seeing privacy and data protection, firstly with its Convention on Human Rights, and then more directly through its Convention on Data Protection 1980, which has given guidance to all its member states, whether or not they have actually acted on it (Council of Europe 1980). The council has two committees concerned with data protection. The Convention Committee is engaged in a long-term follow-up to the 1980 convention and the levels of national implementation that have resulted from it, and its Committee of Experts on Data Protection has worked on a sectoral basis and been the moving force behind the council's various recommendations on data pro-tection.

Recommendations are less 'powerful' than conventions, but still offer important guidance to member states. The following recommendations are particularly pertinent to health and social services provision:

- R(81)1 on automated medical data banks;
- R(83)10 on statistical and research data;
- R(86)1 on personal data used for social security purposes;
- R(87)15 on the use of personal data in the police sector;
- R(89)14 on ethical issues of HIV infection;
- R(91)10 on communication to third parties of personal data held by public bodies.

Recommendation R(91)10 shows a departure from the previous sectoral approach, and shows the council moving more in the direction of the ge-neric across-the-board approach favoured by the European Union.

The European Union

The European Union (previously known as the European Community) has also kept an eye on data protection developments. In 1981 it issued a strong recommendation of its own to its 12 member states that they introduce national legislation to implement the Council of Europe's Convention on Data Protection (*Official Journal of the European Communities*, L.246, 29 Au-gust 1981, p. 31).

In 1990 the EC issued its own Draft Directive on Data Protection to try to bring some harmonisation into the process begun by the Council of Europe. Left to their own devices, a number of EC member states had not intro-duced national legislation, and the European Commission saw the diver-sity of approaches to data protection as a potential obstacle to the flow of data between states in the emerging market structure. The draft directive (reference COM(90)314 Final SYN 287), departing from a sectoral approach, met with some opposition at national level and in the European Parliament, and was revised and re-issued in October 1992 (reference COM(92)422 Final SYN 287).

The UK government is still considering the second draft Directive at the time of writing. The aversion to extending coverage to manual files is apparently breaking down as indicated by the acceptance in the 1994 Code of Practice on Access to Government Information (see page 74).

The Organisation for Economic Co-operation and Development

The OECD, which has a global rather than European membership, has also taken a long-term interest in data protection and offered a forum for discussion of issues arising in privacy and data protection. In 1980 it produced its own set of guidelines on privacy protection and trans-border data flows (OECD 1980) running in parallel to the Council of Europe's Convention.

Today the OECD has a standing Information, Computer and Communications Policy Committee and an Ad Hoc Meeting of Experts on Recent Developments in Data and Privacy Protection, and continues to produce guidance and discussion documents (see, for example, OECD 1994; see also Michael 1994 for a comprehensive overview of all international developments).

5 Access to personal information held by social services agencies

Having considered the methods available to police the circulation of personal information within the welfare network and beyond, we should now turn our attention to the people from whom this information originates, and ask what rights they have to see how 'their' information looks in print or in whatever other form it exists. What rights have they to challenge it, correct it or have it erased?

It has long been a practice amongst some social services staff to share their record-keeping with their clients or service users. This has been seen as a positive working practice that enhances trust and honesty when building professional relationships. The good working relationship is then maintained in using various forms of intervention with the individual or family concerned.

However, these arrangements for allowing access to records in the past, have always been at the discretion of the professional who acts as the holder of the records. Not every social worker was willing to share records. During the 1980s, arguments began to emerge that access to records in this fashion should not be dependent on professional discretion, but should be the right of the subject of the records. The arguments were based on a degree of apprehension about the perceived growth in power of social services agencies, and were put forward in the context of moves towards a generally more open society. Access to subjects' files might help in the regulation of personal information, and at least ensure it was accurate and correct.

As we have also seen in Chapter 1, there have been long-standing debates as to who has the 'ownership' of personal information held on official records. We have noted the qualifications that have to be made to this concept of 'ownership' as applied to personal information. It does not normally have the status of 'intellectual property' to which a copyright can be attached, and the idea of 'ownership' is weakened in the case of personal health information, for example, which may only come to light following the diagnosis of a third party – a doctor – who might equally lay claim to its ownership. Ultimately, files 'belong' to the local authorities, who give out access as appropriate.

Despite these qualifications, the idea that 'personal information' usually comes from the subject of the file and is therefore 'owned' by that person has a powerful appeal. It offers a way of re-establishing integrity over personal information coming from that personal or private zone of life, includes the idea of a person's 'consent', and contrasts with a person's public life. The argument is then put forward that a claim can be made to see that information as of right. The demand is made that 'I want to see "my" file or "my" computer entry.' After all, 'Whose file is it anyway?' (see, for example, Cohen 1982; Frankel and Wilson 1985, and, from the USA, Kimball 1984).

Other arguments for access place the opening of files firmly in the centre of general policies of openness and client empowerment, which: 'emphasise much broader links between access, records and a more equal and participatory practice which demystifies and changes the relationship between people and professionals' (Beresford and Croft 1993, p. 169).

Payne sees this approach to opening files progressing on a series of related fronts. Firstly, there is the role of participation in 'official' activity as part of a democratic society, which in turn makes bureaucracies less oppressive and controlling. The client is empowered within the unequal client–social worker relationship, and is both accorded more respect as a person and helped to achieve a degree of self-realisation. Secondly, sharing files deals with some of the ethical problems that the professionalisation of social work can present (Payne 1989).

By the end of the 1980s, whether or not all these arguments had been fully articulated, statutory rights were in place giving a right of access to social services records, albeit with an element of professional discretion still remaining.

The Graham Gaskin story

Graham Gaskin went into the care of Liverpool City Council Social Services when he was 6 months old, and was in their care until he was 18. Gaskin had numerous care placements during that time, including foster-care, residential care and lodgings found for him by the social services department. After leaving care, a social worker went through Gaskin's file with him and explained some of the background to his life in care.

Gaskin alleged that, because of neglect and mismanagement in care, he had emerged as a 'damaged person', suffering severe psychological injuries and anxiety neurosis. Having sought legal advice, he started a civil action against Liverpool City Council with a view to claiming in respect of personal injuries. Through his lawyers, Gaskin now requested further access to his file to pursue his claim. This time the request was refused, and an application was made in the High Court to force Liverpool City Council to hand over the files.

The application to the High Court was made under the Administration of Justice Act 1970, Section 31, which permits the court to order relevant documents to be passed to a person where there are likely to be subsequent proceedings in a claim for personal injuries. In fact, the High Court denied Gaskin legal access to his file, and when Gaskin appealed against this decision, it was upheld by the Court of Appeal.

The Court of Appeal held that there was a 'public interest' privilege against disclosure, and 'the public interest in the proper functioning of the child care service required that the confidentiality of the child care documents in the possession of the authority should be preserved' (*Gaskin* v. *Liverpool City Council* [1980], 1 WLR 1549). The Gaskin case caused something of a stir in social services circles, and the stirring was taken further by a 'ghosted' autobiography and a BBC 2 television dramatisation of his life in care, starring Paul McGann (published as MacVeigh 1982; see also Fogarty 1982).

Gaskin took his case through to the European Court of Human Rights ('Gaskin fight to file goes to European Court', *Childright*, No. 48, June 1988, p. 5) where it was eventually ruled that the UK had violated Article 8 of the European Convention on Human Rights and should pay Gaskin compensation (*The Gaskin Case* [1990] 1 FLR l67; see also Pickford 1992). By this time, other arrangements for access to files had been put in place.

Circular LAC(83)14

The government's response to this discussion was to issue guidance in the form of a circular encouraging all local authority social services departments to devise access-to-files policies. Such circular guidance has, as we have seen, an uncertain status, but social services directors take it seriously, and they set about devising systems to give people access to their files. One delegate to a BASW conference on the subject asked:

What have we got to hide ... is social work so bad? Have we maltreated and despised our clients? Are our records so bad? On the whole no. We don't have much to be afraid of. ('Keeping information from the client is "cowardly"', *Community Care*, 9 February 1984)

The circular guidance felt that restrictions on access should only take place when necessary to protect third parties, sources of information, confidential judgements made by staff, and in order to protect the client, who might be harmed. Parents who wished access to information on their children were also liable to restrictions, dependent on the circumstances and the child or young person's own wishes (DHSS 1983).

The result was a profusion of policies giving a hesitant non-statutory 'right' of access to files. Many social workers pointed to their good practice, which meant they had been doing this anyway for many years (see, for example, Parry 1985; Flanagan 1986). Others saw the circular as 'one of the most progressive and imaginative to emanate from the Elephant and Castle' (the headquarters of the DHSS) and were eager to report their progress (Butler 1986), whilst the BASW commissioned research to provide 'model procedures' for access arrangements (Ovretveit 1985).

The status of the circular was considered in more detail when the Commissioner for Local Administration investigated a complaint made by a man who was unhappy about the length of time it took to see his files, and the fact that access was denied to certain documents in those files. During the investigation it was revealed that the authority in question, the London Borough of Lambeth, had sought the opinion of counsel on the general legal implications of Circular LAC(83)14. Counsel gave guidance that the circular was, in their view, mandatory, in that local authorities were bound by the Local Authority Social Services Act 1970, Section 7.

The Commissioner for Local Administration had this position confirmed through correspondence with the DHSS: 'the circular is "mandatory" in the sense that authorities must act under the general principles which it sets out' (Commission for Local Administration in England, Complaint No. 956/Y/84, 1986).

Whatever its status, the recourse to circular guidance was not universally welcomed, and opinions were soon being expressed that a statutory basis for access was the only way to establish true rights (Fry 1983). The Children's Legal Centre still found insufficient recognition of children's rights to see what personal information was being kept on them ('Can I see my file?', *Childright*, No. 6, 1984) and found wide variation in policies based on the circular ('79 varieties: policies on access to social work files', *Childright* No. 44, 1988).

Even more bizarre was the acquittal of a person charged with stealing his own file. Kevin Poole had been in the care of Nottinghamshire Social Services, and later stole his file in order to photocopy it. On the basis that the file was costed at £5 and the photocopying had cost £14, it was argued that no gain had been made from the theft, and the original file had even been returned ('Care file "theft": Kev goes free', *Childright*, No. 16, 1985).

The most comprehensive examination of access policies based on the circular comes from Shemmings and his research amongst team leaders and social workers in Essex. Differences of view were found amounting to polarisation, and the advantages of clear policies and good training were emphasised if the authorities were to make the exercise work (Shemmings 1991).

The Education Act 1981, which was implemented in 1983, had meanwhile set a precedent for giving parents a statutory right to see all records and information gathered during their child's assessment for special education. The Campaign for Freedom of Information had put forward its own draft Access to Personal Files Bill (Frankel and Wilson 1985).

The Data Protection Act 1984

Running parallel to these early attempts to open up files (see also Chapter 4) was the gathering concern about computer-held information. Following the Council of Europe Data Protection Convention 1980 the UK had introduced its Data Protection Act 1984 and instituted its first Data Protection Registrar. Not least, the Act gave people the right to see what information was held regarding them on computer.

This right of subject access (Data Protection Act 1984, Section 21) gave legislative backing to Data Protection Act Principle 7. On payment of a fee amounting to not more than £10, data subjects could request disclosure of information held on them within a period of 40 days (some data users do not charge a fee). The impact of these provisions on social services were likely to be minimal because information technology was not being widely used in social services at this time.

In certain circumstances, people might still be denied access to personal information about them despite the overall provisions of the Data Protection Act (Section 29). Personal information held by health or social services agencies – statutory or voluntary – may be withheld if disclosure might prejudice the carrying out of future social work by causing serious harm to the 'physical or mental health or emotional condition of the data subject', or if it might lead to the identification of other people not employed by the agency (Data Protection (Subject Access Modification) (Social Work) Order 1987, SI 1987 No. 1904).

Disclosure should also be withheld if it contains personal information obtained from health professionals, who should first be asked to consent to its disclosure (Data Protection (Subject Access Modification) (Health) Order

1987, SI 1987 No. 1903). Finally, if existing legislation prevents disclosure, such as adoption legislation, the Data Protection Act is again suitably modified to deny subject access (Data Protection (Miscellaneous Subject Access Exemptions) Order 1987, SI 1987 No. 1906; see also DHSS 1987 and Local Authority Social Services letter LASSL (92)9, November 1992). Children may also be denied access, but only if a conscious decision has been made by the authority that the same reasons for which adults might be denied access are applicable, or if the child lacks the capacity to understand (DHSS 1988b, paras 4–10). Special arrangements for mentally disordered people were considered but felt unnecessary (para. 11) (In general, see also *Data Protection Act 1984 Guideline 6: The Exemptions*, available from the Data Protection Registrar).

We might also note at this point a worrying trend that has concerned the Data Protection Registrar – the enforced use of the subject access provisions to *force* people to apply for information held on them. Mostly this is undertaken as a form of 'do-it-yourself' vetting when employers or others request an applicant to access their criminal record from the police computers as a way of screening them. The registrar noted the increased amount of enforced subject access (DPR 1994, p. 24), and also expressed the belief that such enforcement is outside the spirit of the subject access provisions of the Data Protection Act and should be made illegal (DPR 1989). It is not known if social services agencies have ever enforced subject access for potential employees or applicants for other approval, but it might possibly be attractive to the smaller voluntary or private agency which does not have formal disclosure arrangements with the police. Harry Cohen's private member's bill would have given the Secretary of State the power to regulate against enforced subject access and make it a criminal offence.

With the Data Protection Act 1984 seemingly still by-passing the majority of social services case record systems because of their manual rather than computerised nature, in the late 1980s attention was again turned to means of gaining statutory access to these files. A private member's bill from Liberal MP Archie Kirkwood received sufficient support to become the Access to Personal Files Act 1987.

Just as the Campaign for Freedom of Information draft bill had sought to cover a multiplicity of authorities, so Kirkwood's bill threw its net wide. After its passage through the House of Commons, however, it had been watered down to cover only information held by local authority social services and housing authorities.

The Access to Personal Files Act 1987

The Access to Personal Files Act 1987 replaced Circular LAC(83)14. For the first time, clear rights to access were enshrined in law, giving local social services departments a duty to disclose what information they held regarding people, except in particular circumstances. This Act may be referred to as an 'enabling' Act – although it states the general right and makes an attempt to define 'personal information', the power the Act gives to the Secretary of State to make regulations is its main point.

It is in the Act's accompanying Access to Personal Files (Social Services) Regulations 1989 (SI 1989 No. 206) that we find the real substance to the law in practice; the regulations should be read alongside the accompanying circular (DoH 1989c; see also Local Authority Social Services letter from the Department of Health LASSL(92)9, issued November 1992). Separate regulations exist for Scotland (Scottish Education Department 1989b). The 1989 regulations came into force on 1 April 1989.

Regulation 2(1) provides that, in general terms, a local social services authority shall be obliged:

- to inform any individual whether the accessible personal information held by the authority includes personal information of which that individual is the subject;
- to give that individual access to any personal information of which he or she is the subject.

Having assured themselves of the identity of the person applying, and asked questions to enable the location of the material (Regulation 4), social services departments have 40 days in which to meet a request for information (Regulation 6). Subject to the exemptions, the applicant may be not only a user of social services but also a proprietor of a registered home, a foster-parent, 'and other carers who are not employees of the local authority' (DoH, 1989c, Appendix 1, para. 3) if they are seeking information about themselves. The request must be in writing, and as with the Data Protection Act 1984, a fee of up to £10 for this service may be charged (Regulation 3).

The Access to Personal Files Act allows the Secretary of State to make regulations concerning access and including provisions for exemptions or restrictions on disclosure (Section 3(2)(c)). Regulations have duly been drawn up and authorities can deny access if it is felt that:

- it might be damaging to the person concerned;
- it would intrude on the privacy of third parties who could be identified from the file;

- it might reveal personal health information;
- disclosure would hinder criminal detection, etc., or contravene legal provisions.

The regulations gave much greater recognition to information from 'health professionals' (Regulation 8), gave people a right to correct or remove inaccuracies (Regulation 10) and gave specially convened committees of three council members of a local authority the right to 'review' decisions (Regulation 11). The regulations also gave no particular protection to 'confidential judgements' made by social services staff, as provided by Circular LAC(83)14.

The circular had allowed the withholding of information if it revealed social services department staff's 'confidential judgements'. Provisional views and what have sometimes been referred to as 'clinical musings' used to record a definitive plan of intervention could be withheld, although the warning was added that there 'should not be a secondary system of covert records' (DHSS 1983, para. 5(c)). Of course, there were those who argued that it was precisely those pieces of information which were of most use to the users of social services, and they could not see why they should be withheld. The 1989 regulations make no provision in this respect, although the Access to Personal Files Act 1987 itself, in defining 'personal information', says this should include opinion but 'not any indication of the intentions of the authority' with respect to an individual (Section 2(2)). The disclosure of any such intentions might put people and social work plans at risk.

It remains true that 'secondary systems of covert records' would undermine the basic principles of the Access to Personal Files Act, just as selective 'weeding' of files outside the exemption permits would also jeopardise its effect. The regulations make no reference to such phenomena, and there is only tentative guidance from the Department of Health that, although requested files may be routinely amended, 'the information must not be tampered with in order to make it acceptable to the individual' (DoH 1989c, para. 21). We need to examine the four main limitations on disclosure in more detail.

Disclosure that might be damaging to the person concerned

Disclosure can be withheld if it is thought likely to hinder or prejudice social services staff carrying out their functions because it causes 'serious harm to the physical or mental health or emotional condition' of the person concerned (Regulation 9(2)). There is an expectation from the Department of Health that use of this exemption category will be 'most exceptional', and that decisions will need to be made allowing disclosure but still withholding 'just so much of the information as is likely to cause serious harm'. In assessing the 'serious harm' caused, authorities must consider not just 'harm' to the person concerned, but possible harm to others, including social services department staff (DoH 1989c, Appendix 1, paras 55–6).

In practice, the social services department must ask itself two questions in making decisions under Regulation 9(2): would disclosure result in serious harm to the physical or mental health or emotional condition of the person concerned, and if it would, would such disclosure hinder or prejudice the carrying out of social services functions.

In Derbyshire a man challenged the right of a department to withhold information from him because social services staff were not qualified to judge whether he would suffer 'physical or mental health' harm. He argued that this should be a decision made by doctors only. The case was lost in court, where it was ruled that 'emotional condition' must also be assessed, and that, overall, the judgement could be made by social services staff (*R* v. *Derbyshire CC ex parte K*, *The Times* Law Report, 2 May 1994).

Disclosure which might intrude on the privacy of third parties who could be identified from the file

If information might identify third parties, then that information can also be withheld, unless the third party consents, or unless it is obvious that the person seeking access already knows the third party (DoH 1989c, Appendix 1, para. 33). The principle of anonymity for third parties in these circumstances was confirmed in the case of a woman who was the subject of a child abuse investigation instigated by a possible malicious informant. The woman's child was healthy and well cared for, and she wanted to know who the person was who had reported her, as well as being unhappy with the way the investigation was carried out. The case went on appeal to the House of Lords, where it was ruled that there was no right of disclosure. The Law Lords held that it was contrary to 'public interest', because child care agencies relied on such information to carry out their work, and 'sources of information would dry up' if people thought they could be identified (*D* v. *NSPCC* [1978] AC 171 HL(E)). The same arguments were later used to deny Graham Gaskin his file.

Practice today is that third parties must consent to disclosure of their identity. Consent should be obtained in writing within 40 days, and if no consent is received within that period, names should be withheld or disguised. The local authority cannot withhold the names of staff or anyone else it employs or pays to carry out social services functions (DoH 1989c, Appendix 1, para. 39).

Disclosure that might reveal personal health information

Personal health information is defined as coming from two possible sources: from a health professional and from other social work sources.

Personal information held by social services authorities that has been given to them by a 'health professional' can only be disclosed with the consent of that professional (Regulation 8). This means information received from a doctor, dentist, health visitor, nurse or others defined as 'a health professional' in the Schedule to the 1989 regulations. The health professional's consent can be withheld if disclosure is 'likely to cause serious harm to the physical or mental health of the individual' or would reveal the identity of a third party who has not consented to disclosure (Regulation 8(5)). Disclosure that would not cause serious harm can still take place, as can disclosure that disguises individual names or identities.

These additional safeguards concerning personal health information are far in excess of anything to be found in 1983 Circular LAC(83)14. At that time there was only a general exemption to disclosure covering all health professionals, employers, the police, the probation service and other local authority departments. Clearly, these safeguards were considered insufficient by health professionals, and they have taken advantage of the interim consultation period to ensure that greater protective measures have been put in place. They have also distinguished themselves as 'professionals' to be taken into account, rather than their employing authorities, even though it may still be through the 'health authority' that social services make their first request for consent to disclose (Regulation 8(3)). Health employees working in NHS trusts were included in the regulations from 1 August 1991 (Access to Personal Files (Social Services) (Amendment) Regulations 1991, SI 1991 No. 1887).

Health information that has found its way onto social services files but has *not* come from a health service professional is not subject to the same regulation. It is possible that health information may be acquired by social services staff or from another local authority department (DoH, 1989c, Appendix 1, para. 62), and this information is only subject to exemption from disclosure in the same way as non-health-related personal information.

Crime and legal reasons

Information that is on file and would possibly be used in the 'prevention or detection of crime' or 'apprehension or prosecution of offenders' cannot be disclosed (Regulation 9(4)), and neither can any information protected by other legislation – for example, information protected by the Adoption Act 1976, Sections 50 or 51, or the Adoption Agencies Regulations 1983, Regulations 6 or 14 (Regulation 9(6)). If information is held that is considered to be subject to legal privilege, and if disclosure would prejudice an authority's case in terms of prosecution, it can also be withheld (Regulation 9(7)). All three of these circumstances concerning crime, other legal safeguards and legal privilege are additions that were never considered in Circular LAC(83)14.

The position of children and young people seeking access to their files is also not specifically referred to in the 1989 regulations, and we have to turn for guidance to the Department of Health circular that accompanied them. Children and young people may have access in the same way as adults if the authority is satisfied as to the 'child's capacity to make an informed request' (DoH, 1989c, Appendix 1, para. 41). Conversely, parents requesting information on their child must make a declaration that they believe the child does not have the capacity to make an informed request. Social services would be expected to challenge this declaration if their knowledge of the child suggests the child does have the capacity (DoH 1989c, Appendix 1, para. 42). In other circumstances, the exemptions apply as they would to any other applicant for information, and would be withheld, for example, if disclosure to a parent would seriously harm a child (Regulation 9(2)).

Behind these provisions is the thinking implicit in the Gillick decision of 1986, which recognised the rights of young people below the age of 16 to make decisions that affected them, if they were competent to do so (*Gillick v. West Norfolk and Wisbech Area Health Authority* [1986] AC 112). The idea of the 'Gillick-competent' young person was duly enshrined in the Children Act 1989, which requires that children and young people be consulted on decisions wherever practicable.

The 1989 regulations are not retrospective, and people have no *right* to see records kept on them before 1 April 1989, although they are also not *precluded* from seeing them. The regulations make no reference to language difficulties that might be encountered by some people having access to their files, although publicity for the open-access policies is expected to be circulated in languages in addition to English (DoH 1989c, Appendix 1, para. 69). Presumably, the guidance that information may be taken 'to another person for advice' would cover the use of an interpreter if necessary (Appendix 1, para. 19).

The regulations are also clearly designed to complement the provisions for subject access to computer-held information in the Data Protection Act 1984. The regulations address the problem of 'material held in files, card indexes and day books', which does not include video tapes and audio tapes (Appendix 1, para. 5; see also Chapter 3). Presumably, registers fall within the definition of 'card indexes' unless they are held on computer.

Local authorities are required to draw up formal procedures concerning access to files and to identify senior managerial staff who are responsible for making necessary decisions. These decisions would include withholding information, determining a child's capacity to request information, and any decisions concerning files containing both health and social services material which would have to be divided up before access is granted. It is also necessary to keep a record of all instances when information is withheld from people (DoH 1989c, Appendix 1, paras 67–8; see also Dolan 1989).

Regulation 10(1) allows an individual to request that records be corrected or erased if considered inaccurate, and social services departments must comply if satisfied that their information is indeed inaccurate. Any disagreements may be dealt with by putting a written note on the file indicating the nature of the disagreement (Regulation 10(5)); corrected records or records with a written note appended should be shown to the person concerned (Regulation 10(6)). Any continuing disagreements can be referred to a committee of three elected members (see page 98), who will review the decision (Regulation 11). The BASW suggests arbitration could be carried out by independent members of existing complaints bodies (BASW 1992a).

Conclusions

It is still too early to assess the efficacy of local authority policies giving a legal right of access to personal records, and findings are only just beginning to emerge (see, for example, Neville and Beak 1990). In a wider context, access policies fall into line with more openness in social services generally, with better complaints and representation systems and, for example, policies of access to case discussions and child protection conferences for those who are the subject of them. 'Participation' and 'empowerment' have become key words in social work practice, and access to records, integrated into practice, should be able to play its part in these processes.

At the moment, the access policies we know of appear to fall into two camps: on the one hand the formal granting of a civil right to see your file, and on the other the pro-active policy of sharing records as part of an empowerment philosophy. The former is a simple administrative process, and the latter is built into the professional practice of the social worker (Shemmings 1991).

More recent findings from the Social Services Inspectorate suggest that records are still so poorly kept that this in itself becomes a block to subject access. They recommend that access policies should not exist in isolation but be 'part of an overall policy on the content and structure of records' (SSI 1994d, paras 21.1–21.2). As with Bentham's Victorian panopticon, the visibility of today's record keepers, like the original watchers remains obscured.

Allied professions have taken a similar access path with the Education (School Records) Regulations 1989 (SI 1989 No. 1361), giving parents and older pupils access to their educational development records, and the Access to Medical Reports Act 1988 and Access to Health Records Act 1990, opening up further areas of access in relation to health professionals. The Medical Records Act gives access to reports written for employment and insurance purposes, whilst the Access to Health Records Act gives similar rights of access to health professional files to those which exist in relation to social services files, and came into force on 1 November 1991 (see NHS Management Executive 1991).

This sectoral approach to open-access policies – social services, education, health – favoured by the government reflects the approach taken at the international level by the Council of Europe. It is an approach that looks likely to be superseded in future by the more generic across-the-board approach now being put forward by the European Union (see above and Chapter 1).

6 Privacy and the media

Many discussions on the nature of privacy are couched in terms that see privacy in direct opposition to freedom of expression. If freedom of expression is a central value of free Western societies, how do we balance such expression against an individual or corporate desire for privacy? The two positions might be opposite ends of the same continuum, but where do we draw the line?

Much of the contemporary debate on privacy in the UK has been directly related to the media and its intrusiveness, from covert photographs of members of the royal family to exposés of pop stars and politicians. As the battle for increased circulation has intensified, there has been an increased willingness to publish sensational stories and photographs of the private lives of well-known individuals. In turn, the government has grappled with the balancing act necessary to maintain both privacy and freedom of expression (see, for example, Home Office 1990a; Department of National Heritage 1993). Those in favour of freedom of expression suggest that a right of reply might be less constraining than a right to privacy (see, for example, Liberty 1993; Liberty 1994b).

On a lesser scale, social services stories have been good grist to the tabloid circulation mill. Child protection tragedies in particular seem to have all the necessary ingredients of a 'good story', and in turn have led to a situation in which:

Verbal abuse of social workers, bordering on the hysterical, abounds in the popular press ... social workers have not found it easy to cope with such saturating media coverage devoted to each successive child abuse case. (London Borough of Greenwich 1987, p. 134)

For others, it has been the symbolic value of the social worker to a largely right-wing press as incompetent agent of a costly and burdensome welfare state that has given rise to the vitriol (Franklin and Parton 1991).

For present purposes, we need to reflect on the nature of privacy for social services users – and providers – when they come in contact with agencies of the media. Such agencies would include newspapers – both national and local – and radio and television stations. Social services are public services and therefore it is legitimate that interest be shown in them by the media as representatives of the public. The question is, do the media go further than this and infringe the privacy of both service users and providers.

The media and social services users

Journalists most commonly find the sources for their stories in formal places, where an 'official' statement of some kind is made. In terms of social services, we are referring to court hearings, perhaps involving juvenile or adult perpetrators of abuse against children, council meetings, including social services committee deliberations, or public reports made available about various aspects of a local social services agency. These could include 'one-off' special inquiries, SSI reports or even reports from the Commissioner for Local Administration, whose reports are made public.

Journalists are generally less inclined to take informal reports, say, from 'front-line' social services staff, unless they can be confirmed from other formal sources. They are more inclined to take stories direct from service users, where a poor service has been received, and the users have approached the local press almost as a form of complaints mechanism to ensure remedial action from social services departments anxious to avoid bad publicity.

Judicial proceedings are normally open and deliberately in the public domain. Certain safeguards on confidentiality do come into play at times, and not least where children are involved. The United Nations Convention on the Rights of the Child requires that children's 'privacy [must be] fully respected at all stages of [judicial] proceedings' (United Nations 1989, Article 40(2)(b)(v)).

In the UK, both adults and children can have their identity concealed at the point of arrest or while helping police with their inquiries at a police station. The police should only make public statements that 'someone' is being detained or 'helping them with their inquiries' (*R v. Secretary of State for the Home Department ex parte Westminster Press Ltd*, Queens Bench Div. Court, *The Independent* Law Report, 21 January 1992).

If an admission of guilt is forthcoming but the police believe there is no great need to mount a prosecution in the courts, the offender may be cautioned instead. Cautions are used to divert young people and other groups, such as elderly or mentally disordered people, away from the criminal justice system. There seems to be some confusion over the right of the police to make a caution public knowledge, and in one case that received some publicity the *New Law Journal* mused that 'this is, apparently, standard practice in cases which might involve media interest'; the journal itself did not believe there was any case to be made for making cautions public (Editorial, 'Caution and Cautions', *New Law Journal*, 4 February 1994). It has also been argued that, in the case of children, not even social services departments and schools should be notified (Newell 1991, p. 148).

When judicial proceedings become court proceedings, we are moving firmly into the public domain, and courts are open to both press and public to ensure justice is seen to be done. Again, as we have seen, there are restrictions that come into play to preserve the confidentiality of certain categories of people appearing in court.

Children and young people appearing in criminal proceedings before the youth court do so in conditions that impose anonymity. The public are not allowed into the youth court (Children and Young Persons Act 1933, Section 47), and although press representatives are permitted to be present, they are prohibited from publishing details of the young person's name, age, address, school or any other information likely to lead to identification (Section 49, as amended). The same restrictions were later extended to the Crown Court if children and young people were appearing there (Section 10). Similar restrictions apply to television and radio broadcasts (Children and Young Persons Act 1963, Section 57(4)).

This protection of young people from publicity in court builds upon the general duty of the courts to have regard for the welfare of children appearing before them (Children and Young Persons Act 1933, Section 44) and to assist young people to reintegrate into society rather than being indelibly stigmatised.

The courts have the power to lift reporting restrictions if they consider it to be of legitimate public interest. A distinction has to be made between 'public interest' and the 'curiosity of the public' to avoid simply creating headlines for tabloid newspapers, and the lifting of restrictions is generally rare. The murder of a child by another child is the most frequent reason for lifting reporting restrictions (for example, 'The murderer age 12', *Daily Mirror*, 26 October 1988, a front-page story including a large photograph of the convicted child).

Just how courts should arrive at a decision to 'go public' on details of a juvenile has been examined by a judicial review of one such decision to name a young arsonist (*R* v. *Crown Court at Leicester ex parte S* [1992] 2 All

ER 659). The balancing of public interest against children's welfare is sometimes a delicate affair, and perhaps the welfare of the child's family should
also be taken into account. Conflicting views were expressed on the wisdom of lifting restrictions at the end of the trial of two youths convicted for
the murder of 2-year-old James Bulger in 1993, when the impact on the
family was described as 'traumatic' ('Parents devastated by loss of anonymity', *The Independent*, 26 November 1993).

The Calcutt Report on privacy and the press did not reflect on how
decisions should be made to lift reporting restrictions, but did recommend
consolidation of the law to avoid journalists having to sift through the
relevant sections of the legislation (Home Office 1990a, para. 10.3); Calcutt's
follow-up report made the same point in order to avoid 'inconsistencies or
uncertainties' (Department of National Heritage 1993, para. 7.48).

The reporting of crime by newspapers and other forms of media is a
broad subject, and the reader is referred to other texts for a further exposi-
tion (see, for example, Sparks 1992). In practice, some research suggests that
detailed media reporting of local crime is on the decrease. In their study of
local newspapers, Franklin and Murphy found: 'Even at the most basic
level, most courts in the areas we surveyed sit with their press benches
empty' (Franklin and Murphy 1991).

Many newspapers report only the bare details of names and convictions
of people who have appeared in courts often in long lists. Magistrates are
encouraged to facilitate the distribution of such lists to journalists, which
saves the journalists having to sit in court (Home Office 1989). Clearly,
when it comes to juveniles with protected identities, such lists are not very
useful. Journalists then end up reporting on the serious cases rather than
the run-of-the-mill cases that go through a youth court or adult court every
day.

The ADSS has singled out the local press for further criticism when, in
general terms, it persistently links juvenile crime in an area with a local
residential home. In one case, although evidence supported by the police
demonstrated that the home and its residents were not responsible, the
myth continued, with local hostility from the community misdirected at the
children looked after by the local authority (ADSS 1992).

In the summer of 1993 a train of events was put into motion which will
lead to a selective lifting of the veil of privacy over young people caught in
the criminal justice system. A young person remanded to local authority
accommodation absconded before his court hearing. The police considered
him potentially dangerous, and photographs together with personal details
were given to the press, who duly used them (Gliniecki 1993). Although
these actions were strictly against the legal requirements to maintain confidentiality, the Home Secretary announced, within days, his intention to put
such publications on a legal footing. The rationale was the need to protect

the public and assist the re-arrest of the alleged offender as soon as possible (*Hansard*, 11 June 1993, Col. 375 WA).

New powers were added to the Criminal Justice and Public Order Bill which went on to receive its royal assent on 3 October 1994. In future, the press would be able to name a young absconder who is considered a threat to the public, if, with respect to:

a child or young person to whom this paragraph applies who is unlawfully at large, it is necessary to dispense with those requirements [prohibiting press reports] for the purpose of apprehending him and bringing him before a court or returning him to the place in which he was in custody. (Criminal Justice and Public Order Act 1994, Section 49(5)(b))

Under the new Section 49, young people who are 'unlawfully at large', either from a bail arrangement, remand to care or from a care situation following conviction, will be liable to have their identity revealed in the press. The juveniles must have been charged with or convicted of serious offences, which means a violent or sexual offence or an offence which, in the case of an adult, would be punishable with imprisonment for 14 years or more (Section 49(6)). Applications to allow such publicity must be heard in court, and only on application by the Director of Public Prosecutions (Section 49 (7)).

Just how the government intends to square this new power of publicity with the United Nations Convention on the Rights of the Child remains unknown. The government's report on its implementation of the convention made no mention of its intention to introduce the new measures (see DoH 1994d; see also Clarkson and Thomas 1995).

In Family Proceedings, a Magistrates' Court may sit in private (Children Act 1989, Section 97(1)) and prohibitions exist on the publication of details of proceedings:

No person shall publish any material which is intended, or likely to identify –

(a) any child as being involved in any proceedings before a magistrates court in which any power under this Act may be exercised by the court with respect to that or any other child; or
(b) an address or school as being that of a child involved in any such proceedings. (Children Act 1989, Section 97(2))

This protection is effectively widened from the Magistrates' Courts to the High Court and County Court by the Administration of Justice Act 1960, Section 12(1), as amended by the Children Act 1989, Schedule 13, para. 14:

the publication of information relating to proceedings before any court sitting in private shall not of itself be contempt of court except in the following cases, that is to say –

(a)   where the proceedings –

   (i)   relate to the exercise of the inherent jurisdiction of the High Court with respect to minors;
   (ii)   are brought under the Children Act 1989; or
   (iii) otherwise relate wholly or mainly to the maintenance or upbringing of a minor … (Administration of Justice Act 1960, Section 12(1), as amended)

A High Court hearing wardship proceedings, for example, has the power to control press reporting of the case, and the decision to do so is based on a balancing of the need to protect the child from unnecessary distress and to be mindful of the child's welfare against the interests of a free press to report a matter of genuine public interest. The common practice is to allow reporting, with the child's name reduced to an initial, but in theory the balancing that takes place could allow the full reporting of a child's name if it was felt necessary 'to engage the public interest' (*Re W (A Minor)*, Court of Appeal, *The Independent* Law Report, 24 July 1991).

These principles have been most fully laid down in the case of *Re M and N (Wards) (Publication of Information)* [1990] 1 FLR 149, which involved the reporting of two wards of court who had been suddenly removed from foster-care following allegations of sexual abuse. Other courts have had to make similar decisions, such as the reporting of a foster-care placement where the carers of the ward were going to be two gay men (*Re W (A Minor)*, *The Times* Law Report, 13 August 1991, CA) and a case involving a terminally ill baby who was subject to wardship. In the latter case, the court said there had to be a recognised difference between public interest and public curiosity in balancing the need to restrict publicity (*Re C (A Minor)*, No. 2, 1989, *The Times* Law Report, 27 April 1989, CA).

We also need to note another form of court hearing: that provided for people detained in hospital under the Mental Health Act 1983. Detainees can appeal to a Mental Health Review Tribunal to hear their case for discharge from hospital care. Normally, these tribunals are in private, but many sit in public if the patient so requests and the tribunal is satisfied that it would not be contrary to the patient's interests (Mental Health Review Tribunal Rules 1983, SI 1983 No. 942, Regulation 21(1)). Members of the press can attend tribunals held in public, but are subject to restrictions on reporting names and the nature of the proceedings unless the tribunal gives permission (Regulation 21(5)). The press are allowed to report that a named individual has applied to a tribunal, and they can report the final decision of the tribunal (*Pickering* v. *Liverpool Daily Post and Echo Newspapers plc and Others*, Court of Appeal, *The Times* Law Report, 18 January 1990).

The media and social services staff

Social services staff have sometimes felt hounded by journalists in pursuit of a social work 'story', especially when the media scent the blood of a social worker who can be blamed for the death of a child. Apocryphal stories abound of social workers temporarily leaving home to avoid being besieged by the press. Photographers take pictures through office windows or use 'doorstepping' techniques to snatch photographs (see, for example, *Daily Mail*, 4 November 1980 for a 'doorstepped' photograph of a social worker). In its most deceitful form, 'doorstepping' is said to involve a knock on the door, followed by a retreat to the garden gate. When the door is opened, something is said from the gate in a deliberately quiet voice to induce the listener out of the house to hear what is being said, only to be caught in the flash of the camera's bulb.

The BBC itself has been found guilty of 'doorstepping', albeit in a more direct manner than the method described above (*R* v. *Broadcasting Complaints Commission ex parte British Broadcasting Corporation*, 'BBC camera crew invaded subject's privacy', *The Independent* Law Report, 29 October 1992). Its 'Producers' Guidelines' now require it to be a last resort, used only with advance approval from a head of department (BBC 1993, pp. 8–9). The Broadcasting Complaints Commission has a statutory duty to investigate complaints of 'unwarranted infringements of privacy' (Broadcasting Act 1990, Section 143(1)).

The review of press self-regulation has recommended that some forms of physical intrusion should be criminal offences. This would include entering private property without consent, or taking a photograph or recording the voice of someone on private property without consent with intent to obtain personal information with a view to its publication (Department of National Heritage 1993, paras 7.1–7.26). The review also pointed out the possibility of using the Data Protection Act 1984 to protect privacy in these circumstances, as well as to safeguard against misrepresentation. The argument is based on the fact that most newspapers today are produced using electronic technology (paras 7.43–7.46).

7 Exchanging personal information in practice

The purpose of this chapter is to try to locate some of the ideas and concepts discussed earlier in the book in a social work practice context. A number of practice scenarios are considered from the point of view of personal information exchange and confidentiality. An element of selection has entered into the choice of scenarios, and other equally important areas might have been chosen. At times there will be an overlap with subjects already touched on in the preceding chapters.

Child protection

In carrying out their duty to investigate possible child abuse, local authority social workers can collate information from a number of sources. Staff in local education authorities, housing authorities, health authorities and other local authorities have a legal duty to provide information to the social services department engaged in a child protection investigation unless they can argue that the request is unreasonable (Children Act 1989, Sections 47(9)–47(11)); see also Home Office et al. 1991, Part 4). Youth and community workers should also give information to social services on their own initiative if abuse is suspected (DES 1988b, para. 21), and the police should also be forthcoming with information as appropriate. Social services should consult their own records and the Child Protection Register (see Chapter 3).

The ease with which social services can gain access to police information, and especially records of previous convictions, does seem surprising. Within a joint investigation between the two agencies, we might expect an open exchange of information, and such joint investigations are increasingly the norm (see, for example, Metropolitan Police and Bexley Social Services

113

1987; Cleveland Report 1988, pp. 249–50); the arrival of video-recorded interviews has furthered these exercises. What seems less acceptable is when social services check out people when suspicions are more speculative and uncertain. In an allied context, the Home Office has expressed its concern:

> We come across instances where it was a well established unofficial practice – and all the more dangerous for that – for more junior [police] officers to read over extracts of intelligence files to trusted contacts in the relevant local authority departments. (Home Office 1991c, para. 155)

From the opposite perspective, social workers regularly inform the police of instances of child abuse they have come across, especially when it is serious (DoH 1988, para. 30). There is no statutory obligation on them to do this, and indeed discussions prior to the drafting of the Children Act 1989 ruled out the need for any such duty, seeing this more as a matter for the social worker's professional judgement (DHSS 1985, paras 12.3–12.4). In practice, social workers may have their discretion circumscribed by agency policy and procedure (see also Hebenton and Thomas 1992a).

If necessary, social workers can apply for a Magistrate's Order compelling individuals to give them information on the whereabouts of children they are investigating; any incriminating statements made as a result of the order are not admissible in evidence against a person (Children Act 1989, Sections 48(1)–48(2)).

Child protection conferences provide an opportunity to disclose personal information to a series of other practitioners and agencies. The existence of possible child abuse means individual obligations of confidence elsewhere are likely to be breached. Most professional codes of those attending the conference make an exception on confidentiality when it comes to child protection. However, the proceedings of the conferences themselves are carried out in confidence, and the minutes of proceedings are usually headed 'Strictly Confidential' and kept in a secure place (see Home Office et al. 1991, para. 6.35). The courts have endorsed the fact that:

> Records [of child protection conferences] ought not to be lightly exposed to general scrutiny and the work for children jeopardised without careful and cogent reasons for their disclosure. (*Re M (Disclosure of Material)* [1990] 2 FLR 36)

The attendance of parents at child protection conferences, which is now officially encouraged (Home Office et al. 1991, paras 6.11 and 6.23), lends an immediate 'openness' to conferences, but it is still possible to exclude parents for all or part of a conference; if this happens, parents should still be allowed to submit 'a letter or a tape recording' to enable their views to be heard (paras 6.15–6.17).

In many ways, the child protection conference (or any other form of inter-agency conference) is the epitome of the personal information exchange that goes on in the welfare network. An attempt is made to build up as full a picture as possible of the child and his or her circumstances. The police, for example, will disclose previous conviction records and any other relevant information they may have (Hebenton and Thomas 1992b). A focal or key worker will be named and a decision made on the need to add the child's name to the Child Protection Register.

The formal proceedings of a child protection conference will be accompanied by the inevitable off-the-record conversations, especially between those practitioners who know each other well from regular attendance at conferences. Sometimes known as 'below the table' business (Blyth and Milner 1990), these discussions are virtually impossible to police from the point of view of confidentiality. In Cleveland, practitioners in some cases 'had known each other for twenty years or so' and had even exchanged home telephone numbers (Cleveland Report 1988, paras 6.15–6.16).

A debate exists regarding what information is relevant or irrelevant to child protection conferences. Sometimes regular collaboration results in a 'familiarity that breeds contempt for privacy; relevant information about parents may encompass the swapping of almost any snippets of knowledge' (Cooper and Ball 1987, p. 35). One public inquiry found a disagreement between two police officers as to what should and should not have been properly said to a conference (London Borough of Lambeth 1987, p. 148).

If circumstances allow a more lengthy intervention that is strictly non-emergency, recourse may be had to a Child Assessment Order (Children Act 1989, Section 43). Again information must be laid before a magistrate as to why a medical and social assessment is necessary, and again the application would follow a social work exercise in collating information and the convening of a child protection conference. During and after the assessment, social workers should work 'on a multi-disciplinary basis, with pooling of information and consultation on handling the case' (DoH 1991a, para. 4.23).

At another level of child protection, adults leaving prison following sentences for offences against children in the home will be subject to a degree of supervision by the probation service. They will also have their discharge address checked out by social services staff prior to their leaving prison, in order to consider possible child protection issues which may arise (DHSS 1978b). The ex-prisoner cannot be prevented from going to live at any address where there are children, but an adult carer there (usually a woman) may have to decide whether to allow the prisoner to live there and risk possible registration of the children, if not actual removal under the Children Act 1989.

In these circumstances, the former prisoner is described as a 'Schedule 1 offender'. This is a reference to Schedule 1 of the Children and Young Persons Act 1933, which lists the offences it is possible to commit against children. In fact, the procedures described in the previous paragraph should only have applied to Schedule 1 offenders committing offences in the home. In practice it is clear that checks have been consistently made on *all* offenders even if the offence was committed outside the home. Plans were being made in 1994 to legitimate this practice and update the 1978 circular.

This tracking of the Schedule 1 offender after leaving prison tends to occur wherever his name (and, exceptionally, her name) appears. As we saw in the case of the judicial review *R* v. *Devon CC ex parte L* 2 FLR 541 (see pages 87–8), it can even happen when there has been no conviction but only suspicion (see Chapter 4). This means that certain individuals, having served their prison sentence and any subsequent period of supervision, exist in limbo between being a prisoner/supervisee and a fully rehabilitated person with the same rights as any other citizen. Rehabilitation may be distinguished from reform of character, which may or may not have taken place, but arguably, this should not compromise a person's re-integration into society (see McWilliams and Pease 1990).

Young offenders

Social services departments have always been heavily involved with youth justice and young offenders. Sometimes this work sits uneasily alongside other areas of the department's work which is more overtly caring and welfare-orientated. There are those who would like to see it taken out of the hands of social services altogether and put into the charge of a new agency (House of Commons 1993, para. 170).

Working in the field of youth justice puts social workers in a key position regarding personal information and confidentiality at a number of points. Working with people who commit offences invariably, at some time, puts staff in the position of knowing about the commission of an offence and having to decide whether or not to tell the police. Young people will tell them 'in confidence' or workers will assess a situation for themselves and decide that an offence has been committed.

Social services staff are under no specific legal obligation to inform the police if they have knowledge of a crime and who the offender might be (see *Rice* v. *Connolly* [1966] 2 QB 414). They have a common law duty to help the police, and this has been written into the codes of practice of the Police and Criminal Evidence Act 1984, where it appears as a 'civic duty':

All citizens have a duty to help police officers to prevent crime and discover offenders. (Home Office 1991a, Code C, para. 1B)

As we have seen, there are some specific statutory obligations to report crimes in relation to traffic offences and terrorist offences (see page 86), and some reporting may be a necessary prelude to claiming insurance or criminal injuries compensation if a social services officer is the victim of crime. Schools have been advised to notify the police when illegal drugs are found on a pupil or on school premises (DFE 1994a, para. 112; see also DFE 1994b, paras 58 and 60).

In practice, in the normal course of events, social services staff will weigh up the seriousness of an offence and, if necessary, inform the police of their own volition (DoH 1988, para. 30). Failure to notify the police because you have been paid a bribe to keep quiet constitutes an offence (Criminal Justice Act 1967, Section 5(i)), but otherwise a balancing of the information held against the public good that would result from further police action has to be made. Any obligations of confidence are also overridden, in that an 'iniquity' or crime is being disclosed, and therefore action for breach of confidence is unlikely to be successful.

The arrest and detention of a young person in a police station may require a social worker to act in the role of 'appropriate adult'. The police are not entitled to interview young people or other groups of people considered 'vulnerable' without an independent adult being present, unless it is considered particularly urgent or serious by a senior officer. This independent adult is normally the young person's parent, but on occasions it can be the social worker, who has to act as 'appropriate adult' within the meaning of the codes of practice on arrest and detention issued in accordance with the Police and Criminal Evidence Act 1984, Section 66 (Home Office 1991a). At the time of writing, the codes were being revised to take account of the changes introduced by the Criminal Justice and Public Order Act 1994.

Social workers have received various forms of guidance on how to play the role of 'appropriate adult' (see, for example, Thomas 1994a, pp. 105–15; Littlechild 1994). For the purposes of the present discussion, two separate questions are considered.

First, although visiting the young person in a police station, the social worker, as 'appropriate adult', does so in an independent fashion. He or she is not part of the formal 'defence' team but is there to facilitate communication and help the suspect tell a 'story' that is valid and produced without oppression from the police. The social worker may see the young person in private (Home Office 1991a, Code C, para. 3.12) and may balance the need to facilitate communication with the person's right to silence, and what the police may now deduce from that silence (see below).

Second, there has been the vexed question of what the 'appropriate adult' should do if a serious crime is confessed to him or her by the suspect but not in the presence of the police. The question arose in most vivid form when a murder was confessed to an 'appropriate adult' social worker in just such a fashion, and the social worker felt obliged to tell the police when they entered the room to start the interview. Although in this instance the suspect was a vulnerable adult, the dilemmas for the social worker regarding disclosing such information are the same for any suspect (Ogden 1992; see also RCCJ 1993, p. 44). At present, these dilemmas have not been resolved.

In carrying out the role of 'appropriate adult', the social worker must also be aware of the right to silence and the new limits now placed on that right. The changes introduced by the Criminal Justice and Public Order Act 1994, Part III, have led to a reconstituted police caution:

> You do not have to say anything. But it may harm your defence if you do not mention when questioned something which you later rely on in court. Anything you do say may be given in evidence. (Home Office 1995)

The right to silence and the new limitations on it can be placed in the context of privacy and the defence of privacy. The right to silence is the ultimate shield preventing the circulation of personal information against the will of the person who possesses it. To override the right to silence is arguably to seek that personal information without the person's consent and to attack the person's sense of integrity. This idea has been more fully explored by Galligan, who argues that:

> the right of silence serves privacy, which in turn serves this basic sense of personality ... the police have no claim on direct access to that information and it follows that they have no claim on the suspect to lower the shield of privacy. (Galligan 1988)

Following arrest and questioning, and before a young person goes to court, it has become common practice in most localities to discuss his or her circumstances at a liaison panel or bureau, to see if there is any other way of dealing with him or her apart from going to court. These liaison panels are non-statutory bodies made up of police officers, social services staff, and possibly probation service staff, education welfare officers and others. The aim is to divert young people away from the courts and crime through the use of cautions and other measures (see Thomas 1994a, pp. 115–23).

Liaison panels have developed over the last twenty-five years since the Children and Young Persons Act 1969 (see Home Office 1970, paras 92–7). Although generally seen as successful, their future was placed in some doubt by the Home Office in March 1994, when advice was published suggesting fewer cautions should be given to young offenders. The police were further reminded that, 'although it is open to them to seek the advice of multi-agency panels, this should not be done as a matter of course' (Home Office 1994, para. 3).

Whatever the future for liaison panels, as presently constituted they are a forum in which a great deal of personal information about young people and their families is exchanged. When social services department youth justice workers are involved, they may find themselves acting as advocates against a given police proposal. Part of that advocacy will involve the disclosure of personal information on a 'need to know' basis in order to help the panel make a reasoned decision. The problem with crime and anti-social behaviour is that of deciding where exactly the line is drawn to delimit the 'need to know'.

Some social services staff have also seen it as advantageous to approach the Crown Prosecution Service as the final arbiters of which matters go to court and which do not (see, for example, Hardy and Batty 1988). This again allows the youth justice team to disclose confidential information to a third party on a 'need to know' basis. The extent to which disclosure to the CPS or a multi-agency panel is carried out with 'consent' is an unknown variable. Critics have questioned whether this dissemination of personal information is worthwhile:

> It may make the client more vulnerable by making him 'known' to more departments and organisations, and by dispersing and substantially increasing the amount of information about him – information on which any agency may draw in order to confirm its own version, or the generally agreed version, of his 'case'. (Thorpe et al. 1980, p. 128)

As we noted in Chapter 3, the courts are a prime forum for social workers to present personal information to enable other agencies to make more informed decisions. A central part of this exercise is the writing of a pre-sentence report for the court, to assist the sentencing decisions of magistrates or judges. The pre-sentence report is defined in the Criminal Justice Act 1991, Section 3(5).

The writing of pre-sentence reports (PSRs) – and their earlier equivalent, social inquiry reports – has shifted in emphasis over the years from a focus on the offender to a focus on the offence. The PSR should mention sources of information, the facts of the offence and any aggravating or mitigating circumstances, and only then move on to the offender, and finally make some proposals of possible sentences for the court to consider. In completing the section of the PSR which does deal with the offender, social workers (and probation officers) are expected to explore only information relevant to the offence and the likelihood of re-offending, and this would include personal information on:

the offender's explanation for the offence, acceptance of responsibility and feel-ings of guilt or remorse, attitudes, motivation, criminal history, relationships (e.g. family, friends and associates), strengths and skills, and personal problems, such as drugs or alcohol misuse, or financial, housing, employment, medical or psychiatric problems. (Home Office 1992, para. 15)

The final report should be shared with the defendant (unless the court directs this to be impracticable or undesirable because of the defendant's age or understanding), the defendant's parents or guardian, if present, and the defendant's legal representative (Magistrates Courts (Children and Young Persons) Rules, SI 1992, No. 2071, Rules 10(3) and 10(4)). Similar arrange-ments apply to adult defendants (Powers of Criminal Courts Act 1973, Section 46(1)). In the past, social workers have not always taken kindly to legal representatives taking their reports and sometimes quoting them ver-batim as part of the defence. In the case of ill-prepared solicitors, this could amount to the social workers doing their job for them.

Moving away from information privacy to the idea of privacy itself, we need to consider the possible introduction, in the near future, of electronic monitoring of young offenders.

The electronic tagging of offenders – juveniles and adults – has been put forward as a humanitarian way of monitoring people without having to imprison them (see, for example, Home Office 1990b, paras 4.21–4.22). The offender wears a form of bracelet on his or her arm or leg that is electroni-cally linked to a central control system. Various forms of tagging exist but, in essence, movement of the person outside a given area triggers a signal to the controller, who can initiate preventive action to return the person to where he or she should be.

This US idea was imported to the UK in the late 1980s, when trials were carried out on volunteer remand prisoners who wished to avoid being remanded to custody. Although much trumpeted as a new wonder of tech-nology (see, for example, 'Rapists tagged for life', *Today*, 7 July 1989), the trials were generally considered unsuccessful except in a very few cases ('Electronic tags successful in only 7 cases', *Guardian*, 4 April 1990). How-ever, this did not prevent the government including provisions in the Crimi-nal Justice Act 1991 (Section 13) which would enable them to introduce electronic tagging for both remanded and convicted prisoners at some fu-ture point. New field trials were instigated in 1994 in Manchester, Norfolk and Reading ('Home Office plans tagging experiment', *The Times*, 6 May 1994).

Electronic tagging is put forward as an alternative to imprisonment which is cheaper and more humanitarian. Critics say it will be used on those prisoners who would never have gone to prison at all, and will simply be an exercise in 'net-widening'. It is also seen as demeaning in that it reduces people to objects to be monitored, and as being invasive of privacy. Within the household, the early trials found increased domestic violence aimed at the 'prisoner's' spouse or partner (see also Lilley 1990; Nellis 1991).

A new departure in social policy that potentially affects young offenders (and, in fact, all adult offenders) is the increasing involvement of local authorities with people deemed 'public nuisances' and 'poor tenants'. These people may not be convicted offenders, but they draw attention to themselves through their anti-social behaviour. The sort of incidents investigated include disputes over boundaries, excessive noise, racial harassment, inconsiderate car repairs, badly-kept gardens and out of control dogs.

The key figure who intervenes in these situations is the local authority nuisance and harassment officer, who takes witness statements, interviews alleged offenders and issues enforcement notices. In addition, in some areas such as Nottingham, the nuisance and harassment officer contacts 'other relevant agencies such as Environmental Services, Social Services and the police ... for an exchange of information' (City of Nottingham n.d., para. 7). The idea is to build up a composite picture of the offender before taking further action. With the growth of local authority 'private' policing arrangements, we will presumably see more of this inter-agency work in the future (see also 'Sixty councils to seek own police', *Observer*, 28 August 1994).

We might also mention at this stage another category of 'offender' – the so-called 'illegal immigrant'. Following a court judgment in 1993, it has been held that local authorities which have suspicions about a person's immigration status have a duty to report them to the Home Office Immigration and Nationality Department. Although the judgment concerned a housing department, it would seem equally applicable to a social services department (*R* v. *Secretary of State for the Environment ex parte Tower Hamlets London Borough Council* [1993] 3 All ER 439).

Community care

One of the most significant new departures for the personal social services in recent years has been the so-called 'revolution' in community care for elderly, disabled and other vulnerable people. Although the phrase 'care in the community' has been around since the 1970s, the whole process was put on an altogether new footing by the recommendations of the Griffiths Report in 1988 and the ensuing NHS and Community Care Act 1990. Accompanying the Act was a voluminous set of Department of Health guidelines, complemented by more guidance from the Social Services Inspectorate and the Audit Commission. The aim was to challenge the existing structures and culture of social services provision and to replace them with a new enabling status for social services which gave them an assessing and commissioning role that was to be separate from the provision of services. The independent and voluntary sectors were to provide services alongside local authorities and health authorities to give a better package of care with more flexibility and consumer choice – the so-called 'mixed economy of care'.

To bring in the new community care regime, change was needed to challenge existing models of service delivery and accompanying vested interests, to introduce new systems to control the new commissioning role for local authorities, and finally, to improve the traditionally poor working relationships between health service and social services employees. The result would be to replace the old 'services-led' provisions with new 'user needs-led' provisions that would sustain as normal and independent a life as possible, for as long as possible, in the community. The deadline for introduction was 1 April 1993.

Essential to the changes was the introduction of better information management techniques using information technology, devolved operations and better inter-agency co-operation to create a 'seamless service'. It was pointed out that, from the consumer's perspective, the boundaries between primary health care, secondary health care and social care do not really exist. Implicit in the new service regime was a need to exchange personal information on both services and consumers between a number of agencies.

Although the fragmented nature of the system was noted, and the number of agencies involved was to be increased with the addition of the independent and voluntary sector, little attention appears to have been paid to the exchange of personal information and the concept of the 'need to know'. The general assumption appears to have been that this was personal information that could be freely exchanged, and was more or less the same information that would be needed by, say, health or social services, or indeed housing, or anybody else.

As some commentators said on the subject of registers as a means of improving liaison in community care:

> The production of joint registers is often delayed because of problems associated with ownership and confidentiality. The wider use of joint registers, however, offers major opportunities for overcoming the lack of partnership between health and local authorities. (Ballantyne and Symes 1988)

One person who did recognise the implications of community care policies for personal information was the UK Data Protection Registrar. In his 1992 annual report, the registrar noted the increased pressures on the NHS to share information, and not least the pressures that arose 'from links with local authority social services departments arising from the growing emphasis on care in the community' (DPR 1992, p. 10). The registrar also sent a shot across the bows of the NHS with a report on possible infringements of the Data Protection Act involving exchanges between purchasers and pro-viders within the service's own internal market arrangements, let alone exchanges with other agencies (DPR 1993; Cross 1993).

Meanwhile, the Department of Health produced guidance on the new systems, which included the advice that 'a range of methods for sharing ideas and information will be required' (SSI 1991a, para. 4.9). In part, this referred to information on services and policies, but it also meant personal information on the users of community care services:

> If there is a good network of informal communication between agencies, it should rarely be necessary to convene large scale case conferences or review meetings for making decisions about individual needs. (para. 4.10)

More formally, agencies were encouraged to 'develop standard referral and/or assessment schedules and in due course joint databases' (para. 4.9). Once an assessment has been made and a care plan drawn up, this too should be shared with the user 'and all the people who have agreed to provide a service … [and] where other agencies are involved, they should also have a copy of these plans' (SSI 1991b, para. 3.54; see also SSI 1991c, para. 4.5).

Guidance on education and training in the new approaches also fails to make any mention of confidentiality, and the continuing theme is that this is information needed by all agencies, and practitioners only need to know how 'to share knowledge appropriately with other professionals' (CCETSW 1991b, para. 1.5) and be able to pass on 'accurate information about the client's situation and [be] around to help if problems arise' (CCETSW 1992, p. 31). Even the information technology and recording systems of different agencies should be compatible, wherever possible (SSI 1991d, p. 8).

In terms of community care, it is almost impossible to find a recognition in the formal guidance that social information might be different to health information, and that there may not be a 'need to know'. Occasionally, there are acknowledgements that information exchanged should be 'with the consent of the person concerned' (SSI 1991d, p. 9), or that merged client information systems would need to address issues of confidentiality (Audit Commission 1992, para. 95). Only in Northern Ireland is there specific guidance on the professional duty of confidentiality, and that, in making comprehensive community care assessments, 'staff should always bear in mind the need to observe the rules of confidentiality' (SSI (NI) 1991, paras 15.1–15.3). Elsewhere, with the exhortation that 'we cannot stress too strongly the continued need for collaboration and joint working in all areas' (SSI 1993c, para. 9), the question of confidentiality has been by-passed. The search for technical solutions appears to have obscured the need to address the more structural barriers to a 'seamless service'.

In a policy statement, the British Association of Social Workers makes no reference to confidentiality but does lay down what it expects from health professionals in the way information is exchanged (BASW 1992b).

8 Conclusions

Privacy and information privacy should be at the forefront of all professional thinking within the social services. Both are certainly dealt with in formal ethical codes of practice, and efforts are made to uphold them. Renewed efforts will be needed in the face of continuing developments in technology and in the move toward more inter-disciplinary work which necessitates the sharing of personal information.

The use of technology as part of the constant striving for more effective services that also 'protect' the public and 'protect' the client seems to be in steady conflict with a right to privacy. In Chapter 1 we referred to the electronic monitoring of older people who might wander off from residential care. The Director of Social Services for Humberside described the moves as part of a 'personal safety system' that was preferable to locked wards. Despite a hail of criticism that tagging was demeaning, the trials still went ahead ('Humberside goes ahead with tagging', *Community Care*, 23 February 1989, p. 5). Technical difficulties were seen as the real obstacle, rather than moral arguments, and these difficulties included the problem of how to stop passing taxis setting off the alarms ('Tag Hitch', *Community Care*, 7 September 1989, p. 3)!

Undeterred by the privacy arguments and the demeaning of human dignity, electronic tagging of older people remains on some people's agendas. Doctors at the John Radcliffe Hospital in Oxford again gave humanitarian reasons for introducing clinical trials to test some form of electronic transmitter attached to a person's clothing, and cited market research by a major electronics company suggesting a potential European market worth £160 million (McShane et al. 1994).

The Royal College of Nursing has argued that electronic tagging should never be a substitute for good nursing care or adequate staffing levels, but accepts that, if it is necessary, it should be a short-term exercise to start with, and if long-term, should be regularly reviewed (RCN 1994). Counsel and Care, a pressure group for elderly people, have been amongst the strongest critics of tagging, and have called for a much fuller public discussion, clarification of the law and a stronger lead from the Department of Health (Counsel and Care 1993).

In terms of protecting the public, it is the electronic monitoring of criminals that is very much on the current agenda. Here technology is used to identify not only a person but his or her every movement in the community. The very idea of such technology has been welcomed in the tabloid press (see, for example, Editorial, *Today*, 7 July 1989).

Tagging has also been proposed in the wake of much-publicised offences against children. Following the murder of 2-year-old James Bulger in February 1993 after he had been lured away from a shopping centre in Liverpool, proposals were made to issue electronic tags to link children automatically with their parents should they become separated ('Shops study electronic tags to save children', *Daily Telegraph*, 5 November 1993). Tags have also been used to prevent the abduction of children from maternity wards following the case of Abbie Humphreys in the summer of 1994 ('Hospitals warned on baby-theft risk', *Guardian*, 18 October 1994). Walsall and Gateshead were amongst those health authorities who invested heavily in electronic devices to prevent abductions.

Other technical devices with the potential to invade privacy include the penile plethysmograph from the USA, used in some treatment programmes with male sex offenders. This is a small, mercury-filled loop which is placed over the subject's penis to measure his state of sexual arousal when confronted by given stimuli such as photographs of children. According to reports, offenders found the process of putting the plethysmograph on 'extremely embarrassing' (Sampson 1994, p. 122) and its use was banned in UK prison hospitals in 1980 (Howard League 1985, p. 98).

Within the office, the introduction of electronic mail (or e-mail) reduces telephone time and photocopying time because information is immediately available on computer screen, as well as reducing paper and postal costs. In terms of social services spread across a given locality, it provides essential links between staff in geographically dispersed offices.

Computer-readable data cards – sometimes known as 'smart cards' – provide an immediate, portable record that a person can produce to be read by a computer terminal. The cards and equipment allow new information to be added but do not allow information to be erased. The health service has already run trials with patient data cards in Exmouth, South Devon and the Grampian Health Board in Scotland. Patients may hold their own cards as part of the 'record-sharing' philosophy.

Smart cards, computers, electronic monitoring, video, e-mail, faxes and photocopying all demonstrate the growth of technology in the caring professions. To some extent, the new devices 'feed off each other', as, for example, in security devices that allow entrance only after video surveillance and the computer reading of a smart card. In effect, our data or electronic image becomes as important as our real selves, as an extension of Rule's idea that we almost inhabit two worlds at once (Rule 1973, p. 13). Privacy as we have known it becomes less important as 'strangers' become identified and classified.

All of these new developments in technology will question our future concept of privacy in a social services context and on a wider front. We should note, for example, the national debate on identification cards for everyone, telephones that warn who is calling, the spread of video-camera surveillance in public areas in the name of crime prevention, and the creation of a national databank of DNA samples taken from 'serious offenders'. Neighbourhood Watch, Truancy Watch and all the other forms of 'Watch', further challenge our traditional understanding of privacy in public areas. Public order legislation and policing are reconstituted to try to regulate the space that makes up the physical public domain. An intrusive press creates inroads into what was previously considered private, as the idea of the 'public interest' gets stretched in new directions, and everyone seems 'entitled' to their 15 minutes of fame, whether they want it or not. If you wish to stay anonymous and still communicate with the world you can do so by getting 'wired' to electronic communications systems like Internet that make up the so-called 'information super-highway'. Ultimately, these new developments offer a world-wide web delivering instant data, television and other services to millions of people in their own homes or offices by use of optical fibre links.

In the UK, these visions of the future must be imposed on our existing traditions that favour freedom over privacy and that exist within an unwritten constitution rather than any Bill of Rights. Technology has also advanced within a free-market culture that discourages any forms of regulation and encourages a simple 'hands-off' approach to allow initiative its full rein. Wider questions of morality and rights then have to try to reimpose themselves on systems already up and running.

In social services we are seeing the rethinking of bureaucracies for welfare in terms of information technology 'freeing' workers from traditional lines of management, as budgets and decision-making gets devolved. At the same time, we see services no longer being directly provided but being packaged out to the private and voluntary sectors for provision by a range of different agencies. Information technology assists the local authority, for example, to control and enable this 'mixed economy of care'. For those who might fall through the gaps of care provision we develop new monitoring systems, such as supervision registers for some mentally disordered people, child protection registers or other tracking devices to keep an eye on those we think need care (or control) in the city of strangers.

The statutory regulation of the movement of personal information has initially focused on computer-held information and taken a sector-by-sector approach. In the future we are going to see a move toward regulating all forms of personal information processing, whether this is by electronic methods or traditional manual systems. The sectoral approach also looks set to give way to a more general approach that goes beyond one agency or system. Social services seems set to be swept up in these changes.

The regulating of personal information movement at a non-statutory level has a less predictable future within social services. There is already uncertainty as to how circular guidance, for example, is followed by local authorities. Circular LAC(88)17 (DoH 1988) is a prime example of a circular, that appears, at an anecdotal level, to be very hit and miss in its application.

At a professional level of regulation we are still beset by the problems of whether or not social work and social services staff claim professional status for themselves. With the British Association of Social Workers and the Social Care Association claiming only a minority of their potential membership, we await with uncertainty the moves toward a General Social Services Council. Elsewhere, the probation service is told it can lose its social work educational base ('Anger sparked by changes to Probation Officers' training', *Community Care*, 2–8 March 1995, p. 4) and the Prime Minister John Major tells us there is 'little or no public support for the social orthodoxies of the 1960s which still hold sway in social work training' (10 Downing Street, Press Notice, 9 September 1994). The continuation of such moves will only weaken the professional line on maintaining appropriate confidentiality.

Some of this exchange of personal information – whether effectively regulated or not – has now been formalised so that it no longer represents a mutual exchange between practitioners of equal status but effectively requires social workers to produce information to other agencies for them to act on. Social workers need to appreciate the extent to which their work now involves the social production of knowledge for other agencies with non-social work agendas.

Bibliography

ADSS (Association of Directors of Social Services) (1992) Evidence to the Calcutt Inquiry, President of ADSS, Kent, 4 November.

Age Concern (1986) *The Law and Vulnerable Elderly People*, Age Concern, Mitcham.

Aldhouse, F.G.B. (1991) 'UK Data Protection – Where are we in 1991?', *Yearbook of Law Computers and Technology*, Vol. 5.

Algie, J. (1986) 'Weighing up Priorities', *Community Care*, 11 September, pp. 18–20.

AMA (Association of Metropolitan Authorities) (1994) *Consultation on Supervision Registers*, AMA, London.

Audit Commission (1992) *Community Care: Managing the Cascade of Change*, London, HMSO, para. 95.

Baldwin, R. (1988) 'Trend to Coded Practice', *Guardian*, 30 May.

Ballantyne, R. and Symes, D. (1988) 'Building information bridges', in Stockford (1988).

Barclay Report (1982) *Social workers: Their role and tasks*, Bedford Square Press, London.

BASW (British Association of Social Workers) (1971) *Discussion Paper No. 1: Confidentiality in Social Work*, BASW, London.

BASW (British Association of Social Workers) (1982) *Data Protection: Government proposals for legislation*, BASW, Birmingham.

BASW (British Association of Social Workers) (1983) *Effective and Ethical Recording*, BASW, Birmingham.

BASW (British Association of Social Workers) (1986) *A Code of Ethics for Social Work*, BASW, Birmingham.

BASW (British Association of Social Workers) (1990) *Proposed Legislation: Adults at risk*, BASW, Birmingham, 26 September.

BASW (British Association of Social Workers) (1992a) *Graham Gaskin: Social Work Records*, BASW, Birmingham, 16 April.

BASW (British Association of Social Workers) (1992b) *Users of Health and Social Services – Exchanging Information*, BASW, Birmingham.

Bauman, Z. (1987) *Legislators and Interpreters*, Polity Press, Cambridge.

Bayley, M. (1989) 'Values in locally based work', in Shardlow (1989).

Bayley, M., Parker, P., Seyd, R. and Tennant, A. (1987) *Practising Community Care*, University of Sheffield/*Community Care*.

BBC (British Broadcasting Corporation) (1993) 'Producers' Guidelines', BBC, London.

Beetham, D. (1987) *Bureaucracy*, Open University Press, Milton Keynes.

Benn, S.I. and Gaus, G.F. (eds) (1983) *Public and Private in Social Life*, Croom Helm, London.

Bennett, C.J. (1992) *Regulating Privacy*, Cornell University Press, Ithaca, New York.

Bennett, T. (1990) *Evaluating Neighbourhood Watch*, Gower, Aldershot.

Beresford, P. and Croft, S. (1993) *Citizen Involvement*, BASW/Macmillan, London.

Biestek, F.P. (1961) *The Casework Relationship*, George Allen and Unwin, London.

Blyth, E. and Milner, J. (1990) 'The process of inter-agency work', in Violence Against Children Study Group (1990).

BMA (British Medical Association) et al. (1994) *A Bill Governing Use and Disclosure of Personal Health Information*, July (published jointly with 11 other participating bodies), BMA, London.

BMA, GMSC, HEA, Brook Advisory Centres, FPA on RCGP (1993) *Confidentiality and people under 16*.

Borkowski, M., Murch, M. and Walker, V. (1983) *Marital Violence: The community response*, Tavistock Publications, London.

Bourn, C. and Benyon, J. (eds) (1983) *Data protection: Perspectives on information privacy*, University of Leicester.

Brandon, D. (1975) 'Clients have a right to hope for better Privacy than this', *Community Care*, 23 April.

Bridge, A. (1992) 'A nation of secret policemen', *The Independent*, 10 February.

Butler, T. (1986) 'Opening up', *Social Work Today*, 28 April.

Butrym, Z. (1976) *The Nature of Social Work*, Macmillan, London.

Carter, P., Jeffs, T. and Smith, M. (eds) (1990) *Social Work and Social Welfare Yearbook* 2, Open University Press, Buckingham.

CCETSW (Central Council for Education and Training in Social Work) (1989) *Multidisciplinary Teamwork*, CCETSW, London.

CCETSW (Central Council for Education and Training in Social Work) (1991a) *DipSW: Rules and Requirements for the Diploma in Social Work*, (2nd edn), CCETSW, London.

CCETSW (Central Council for Education and Training in Social Work) (1991b) *Assessment, Care Management and Inspection in Community Care*, CCETSW, London.

CCETSW (Central Council for Education and Training in Social Work) (1992) *Contracting and Case Management in Community Care*, CCETSW, London.

Centre for Policy on Ageing (1984) *Home Life: A Code of Practice for residential care*, Centre for Policy on Ageing, London.

Chamberlain, L. (1987) 'Secret taping of clients on telephone widely criticised', *Community Care*, 5 February.

Chancellor of the Duchy of Lancaster (1993) *Open Government*, Cm 2290, HMSO, London.

Citizen's Charter (1991) The Citizen's Charter, Cm 1599, HMSO, London.

Citizen's Charter (1994) *Code of Practice on Access to Government Information*, HMSO, London.

City of Nottingham (n.d.) *The role of the nuisance and harassment officers*, Housing Department, Nottingham.

Clarkson, M. and Thomas, T. (1995) 'Press Reports of Young Offenders under Section 49', *Childright*, No. 113, January–February, p. 5.

CLC (Children's Legal Centre) (1988) *Child Abuse Procedures – the child's viewpoint*, CLC, London.

Cleveland Report (1988) *Report of the Inquiry into Child Abuse in Cleveland 1987*, Cm 412, HMSO, London.

Clough, R. (1982) *Residential Work*, BASW/Macmillan, London.

Cockburn, J. (1990) *Team Leaders and Team Managers in Social Services*, Social Work Monographs, University of East Anglia.

Cohen, R. (1982) *Whose file is it anyway?*, NCCL, London.

Cohen, S. (1985) *Visions of Social Control*, Polity, Cambridge.

Cooper, D.M. and Ball, D. (1987) *Social Work and Child Abuse*, BASW/Macmillan, London.

Corby, B. (1987) *Working with child abuse*, Open University Press, Milton Keynes.

Council of Europe (1950) *European Convention on Human Rights*, Council of Europe, Strasburg.

Council of Europe (1980) *Convention for the Protection of Individuals with regard to Automatic Processing of Personal Data*, Strasburg Convention No. 108, Council of Europe, Strasburg.

Counsel and Care (1991) *Not such private places*, Counsel and Care, London.

Counsel and Care (1993) *People not Parcels*, Counsel and Care, London.

Cross, M. (1993) 'Big Brother', *Health Services Journal*, 15 April, pp. 20–22.

Culf, A. (1990) '3,000 names on Yard Paedophile Register', *Guardian*, 28 July.

Davidson, C. (1991) 'Will computers hold key to mental hospitals?' *New Scientist*, 2 November, p. 22.

Dawson, J. (1983), 'Data Protection and the medical profession', in Bourn and Benyon (1983).

Department of National Heritage (1993) *Review of Press Self-Regulation*, Cm 2135, HMSO, London.

DES (Department of Education and Science) (1988a) *Regulations on the Keeping and Disclosure of Pupil Records: A consultative document*, HMSO, London.

DES (Department of Education and Science) (1988b) *Working Together for the Protection of children from abuse: procedures within the Education Service*, Circular 4/88, HMSO, London.

DFE (Department for Education) (1994a) *The Education of Children with Emotional and Behavioural Difficulties*, Circular 9/94, HMSO, London.

DFE (Department for Education) (1994b) *Drugs prevention and Schools: draft circular*, November, HMSO, London.

DHSS (Department of Health and Social Security) (1974a) *Report of the Committee of Inquiry into the Care and Supervision provided in relation to Maria Colwell*, HMSO, London.

DHSS (Department of Health and Social Security) (1974b) *Non-accidental injury to children*, Circular 74(13), HMSO, London.

DHSS (Department of Health and Social Security) (1977) *Records in Social Services Departments: A Development Group Project Report*, HMSO, London.

DHSS (Department of Health and Social Security) (1978a) *Social Service Teams: The Practitioner's View*, HMSO, London.

DHSS (Department of Health and Social Security) (1978b) *Release of Prisoners Convicted of Offences Against Children in the Home*, Circular LAC(78)22, HMSO, London.

DHSS (Department of Health and Social Security) (1980a) *The Report of the Committee of Inquiry into the Case of Paul Steven Brown*, Cmnd 8107, HMSO, London.

DHSS (Department of Health and Social Security) (1980b) *Child Abuse: Central Register Systems*, Circular LASSL(80)4, HMSO, London.

DHSS (Department of Health and Social Security) (1982) *Child Abuse: A Study of Inquiry Reports 1973–1981*, HMSO, London.

DHSS (Department of Health and Social Security) (1983) *Personal Social Services Records: Disclosure of Information to Clients*, Circular LAC(83)14, HMSO, London.

DHSS (Department of Health and Social Security) (1985) *Review of Child Care Law*, HMSO, London.

DHSS (Department of Health and Social Security) (1986) *Confidentiality of Personal Social Services Records*, draft Circular CFR/22, HMSO, London.

DHSS (Department of Health and Social Security) (1987) *Data Protection Act 1984 Social Work etc. Orders: Individuals' Rights of Access to Information*, Circular LAC(87)10, HMSO, London.

DHSS (Department of Health and Social Security) (1988a) *Report of the Committee of Inquiry into the Care and After-care of Miss Sharon Campbell*, Cm 440, HMSO, London.

DHSS (Department of Health and Social Security) (1988b) *Data Protection Act 1984 Social Work etc. Orders: Individuals' Rights of Access to Information*, Circular LAC(88)16, HMSO, London.

DoE (Department of the Environment) (1990), *The national code of local government conduct*, Circular 8/90.

DoH (Department of Health) (1988) *Personal Social Services: Confidentiality of Personal Information*, Circular LAC(88)17.

DoH (Department of Health) (1989a) *Homes are for living in*, HMSO, London.

DoH (Department of Health) (1989b) *The Care of Children: Principles and Practice in Regulations and Guidance*, HMSO, London.

DoH (Department of Health) (1989c) *Access to Personal Files Act 1987: Access to Personal Files (Social Services) Regulations*, Circular LAC(89)2.

DoH (Department of Health) (1991a) *The Children Act 1989, Guidance and Regulations Vol. 1: Court Orders*, HMSO, London.

DoH (Department of Health) (1991b) *The Children Act 1989, Guidance and Regulations Vol. 4: Residential Care*, HMSO, London.

DoH (Department of Health) (1991c) *Child Abuse: A Study of Inquiry Reports 1980–1989*, HMSO, London.

DoH (Department of Health) (1991d) *The Children Act 1989, Guidance and Regulations Vol. 2: Family Support, Day Care and Educational Provision for Young Children*, HMSO, London.

DoH (Department of Health) (1991e) *The Children Act 1989 Guidance and Regulations, Vol. 3: Family Placements*, HMSO, London.

DoH (Department of Health) (1991f) *The Children Act 1989 Guidance and Regulations Vol. 6: Children with Disabilities*, HMSO, London.

DoH (Department of Health) (1991g) *Registered Blind and Partially Sighted People at 31 March 1991, England*, Local Authority Statistics A/F 91/7, HMSO, London.

DoH (Department of Health) (1991h) *Care Management and Assessment Practitioners' Guide*, HMSO, London.

DoH (Department of Health) (1992) *Registers of the Deaf and Hard of Hearing at 31 March 1992, England*, Local Authority Statistics A/F 92/20, HMSO, London.

DoH (Department of Health) (1993a) *Code of Practice: Mental Health Act 1983*, HMSO, London.

DoH (Department of Health) (1993b) *Guidance on permissible forms of control in children's residential care*, HMSO, London, April.

DoH (Department of Health) (1993c) *Children Act 1989: A report*, Cm 2144, HMSO, London.

DoH (Department of Health) (1994a) *Children and Young People on Child Protection Registers Year Ending 31 March 1993, England*, Local Authority Statistics A/F 93/13, HMSO, London.

DoH (Department of Health) (1994b) *Draft Guide to arrangements for inter-agency care and protection of severely mentally ill people*, HMSO, London, October.

DoH (Department of Health) (1994c) *Confidentiality, Use and Disclosure of Personal Health Information (Draft Guidance)*, HMSO, London, August.

DoH (Department of Health) (1994d) *The United Kingdom's First Report to the UN Committee on the Rights of the Child*, HMSO, London.

Dolan, P. (1986) 'Protecting Personal Privacy', *Community Care*, 24 July.

Dolan, P. (1989) Access to Personal Files: A Practical Guide to the Act, *Social Work Today*, 30 March.

Donajgrodski, A.P. (ed.) (1977) *Social Control in Nineteenth Century Britain*, Croom Helm, London.

Dourado, P. (1991) 'Good cause for complaint', *Community Care*, 13 June, pp. 16–17.

Dovey, H.O. (1986) 'Why national registration had to go', *Public Administration*, Vol. 64, p. 459.

Downey, R. (1990) 'Fears over disclosure ruling', *Social Work Today*, 14 June.

DPR (Data Protection Registrar) (1985) *Codes of Practice – A Preliminary Policy Statement*, Guidance Note No. 1.

DPR (Data Protection Registrar) (1986a) *Codes of Practice – Second Explanatory Statement*, Guidance Note No. 6.

DPR (Data Protection Registrar) (1986b) *Implementing the Data Protection Act 1984: Policies and Views of the Registrar*, Guidance Note No. 7.

DPR (Data Protection Registrar) (1989) *The use of subject access provisions of the Data Protection Act to check the criminal records of applicants for jobs or licences*, Guidance Note No. 21.

DPR (Data Protection Registrar) (1990) *Sixth Report of the Data Protection Registrar*, HMSO, London.

DPR (Data Protection Registrar) (1992) *Eighth Report of the Data Protection Registrar*, HMSO, London.

DPR (Data Protection Registrar) (1993) *NHS Contract Minimum Data Sets*, Data Protection Registrar, Wilmslow, Cheshire, February.

DPR (Data Protection Registrar) (1994) *Tenth Report of the Data Protection Registrar*, HMSO, London.

Edelman, M. (1977) *Political Language: Words that Succeed and Policies that Fail*, Academic Press, New York.

Feldman, D. (1993) *Civil Liberties and Human Rights in England and Wales*, Clarendon, Oxford.

Fennel, P. (1989) 'Falling through the legal loopholes', *Social Work Today*, 30 November.

Fido, J. (1977) 'The Charity Organisation Society and social casework in London 1869–1900', in Donajgrodski (1977).

Flaherty, D.H. (1989) *Protecting Privacy in Surveillance Societies*, University of North Carolina Press, Chapel Hill, N.C.

Flanagan, R. (1986) 'When a family shares your records', *Social Work Today*, 20 January.

Fogarty, M. (1982) 'The right to know', *Social Work Today*, Vol. 13, No. 18, 12 January.

Forbes, J. and Thomas, T. (1989) 'Choice, consent and social work practice', *Practice*, Vol. 3, No. 2, pp. 136–47.

Foreman, D.M. and Farsides, C. (1993) 'Ethical use of covert videoing techniques in detecting Munchausen syndrome by proxy', *British Medical Journal*, No. 307, pp. 611–13.

Foucault, M. (1977) *Discipline and Punishment*, Allen Lane, London.

Frankel, M. and Wilson, D. (1985) *I want to know what's in my file*, Campaign for Freedom of Information, London.

Franklin, B. and Murphy, D. (1991) 'Local rags with a reputation in tatters', *The Independent*, 30 October.

Franklin, B. and Parton, N. (eds) (1991) *Social work, the Media and Public Relations*, Routledge, London.

FRG (Family Rights Group) (1987) *Confidentiality of Personal Social Services Records*, FRG, London.

Fry, A. (1983) 'Files Circular was too hasty – AMA', *Community Care*, 1 September.

Fry, A. (1993) 'Registering Concern', *Guardian*, 10 November.

Galligan, D.J. (1988) 'The Right of Silence Reconsidered', *Current Law Problems*, Vol. 41, pp. 69–92.

Ganz, G. (1987) *Quasi-legislation: Recent developments in secondary legislation*, Sweet and Maxwell, London.

General Social Services Action Group (1992) *General Social Services Council: Consultation Papers*, National Institute for Social Work, London.

Gibson, B., Cavadine, P., Rutherford, A., Ashworth, A. and Harding, J. (1994) *The Youth Court: One year onwards*, Waterside Press, Winchester.

Gilham, C. (1994) 'Disclosure of Social Services Files to the Defence in Criminal Proceedings', *Family Law*, Vol. 24, January, pp. 33–7.

Glastonbury, B. (1985) *Computers in Social Work*, BASW/Macmillan, Basingstoke.

Gliniecki, A. (1993) 'Newspapers "defy law" in reports about boy suspect', *The Independent*, 9 June.

GMC (General Medical Council) (1994) *Annual Report 1993*, GMC, London.

Gostin, L. (1986) *Mental Health Services – Law and Practice*, Shaw and Sons, London.

Griffiths Report (1988) *Community Care: Agenda for Action*, HMSO, London.

Gurrey, M. (1990) 'Anxiety Overload', *Community Care*, 15 November, pp. 18–20.

Gurry, F. (1984) *Breach of Confidence*, Clarendon Press, Oxford.

Hadley, R., Cooper, M., Dale, P. and Stacey, G. (1987) *A community social worker's handbook*, Tavistock, London.

Hall, C. (1994) 'NHS Chiefs accused of ignoring privacy', *The Independent*, 27 July.

Hallett, C. and Stevenson, O. (1980) *Child Abuse Aspects of Inter-professional Cooperation*, George Allen and Unwin, London.

Handscomb, M. (1991) 'On film, and fodder for fantasies', *The Independent*, 13 September.

Harbridge, E. (1983) 'Doctors lose vote to withhold data from the SSD's', *Community Care*, 30 June.

Hardingham, S. (1986) 'We've got them – now what do we do with them?', *Social Services Insight*, 22 February.

Hardy, C. and Batty, C. (1988) 'Making liaison with the CPS work for your clients', *Social Work Today*, 25 August.

Harris, T. (1984) 'Open Secrets', *Community Care*, 27 September, pp. 22–3.

Haviland, L.K. and Haviland, J.B. (1983) 'Privacy in a Mexican Indian village', in Benn and Gaus (1983).

Hayes, M. (1992) 'R v. Devon County Council ex parte L: Bad practice, bad law and a breach of human rights?' *Family Law*, Vol. 22, June, pp. 245–51.

Hearn, B. (1991) 'Registration or Protection?', *Community Care*, 13 June.

Hebenton, B. and Thomas, T. (1992a) 'The police and social services departments in England and Wales: the exchange of personal information', *Journal of Social Welfare and Family Law*, No. 2, pp. 114–26.

Hebenton, B. and Thomas, T. (1992b) 'The police attendance at child protection conferences: A reappraisal', *Children and Society*, Vol. 6, No. 4, pp. 38–50.

Hebenton, B. and Thomas, T. (1993) *Criminal Records: State, citizen and the politics of protection*, Avebury, Aldershot.

Henderson, M. (1994) 'The deceit that led us to Sandra', *Guardian*, 20 August.

Hewson, B. (1993) *Seizure of confidential material - PACE special procedure*, Butterworths, London.

HFEA (Human Fertilisation and Embryology Authority) (1993) *Code of Practice* (2nd edn.), HFEA, London.

Hill, C. (1970) *God's Englishman*, Wiedenfeld and Nicolson, London.

Home Office (1970) *Part 1 of the Children and Young Persons Act 1969: A guide for courts and practitioners*, HMSO, London.

Home Office (1975a) *Computers and Privacy*, Cmnd 6353, HMSO, London.

Home Office (1975b) *Computers: Safeguards for Privacy*, Cmnd 6354, HMSO, London.

Home Office (1982) *Data Protection: the Government's proposals for legislation*, Cmnd 8539, HMSO, London.

Home Office (1989) *Press access to court lists and the register of decisions in Magistrates Courts*, Circular 80/1989, HMSO, London.

Home Office (1990a) *Report of the Committee on Privacy and Related Matters*, Cm 1102, HMSO, London.

Home Office (1990b) *Crime, Justice and Protecting the Public*, Cm 965, HMSO, London.

Home Office (1991a) *Police and Criminal Evidence Act 1984 (s66) Codes of Practice*, HMSO, London.

Home Office (1991b) *Misuse of witness statements in sexual offences cases: A consultation paper*, HMSO, London.

Home Office (1991c) *The National Collection of Criminal Records: Report of an Efficiency Scrutiny*, HMSO, London.

Home Office (1992) *National Standards for the Supervision of Offenders in the Community*, HMSO, London.

Home Office (1993) *Disclosure of Criminal Records for Employment Vetting Purposes*, Cm 2319, HMSO, London.

Home Office (1994) *The cautioning of offenders*, Circular HOC18/1994, HMSO, London.

Home Office (1995) 'Michael Howard announces new police caution', (news release), 30 January.

Home Office, DFE, DoH and Welsh Office (1993) *Protection of Children: Disclosure of criminal background of those with access to children*, Circular HOC47/93, HMSO, London.

Home Office/DHSS (1987) *Supervision and After Care of Conditionally Discharged Restricted Patients: Notes for the Guidance of Social Supervisors*, HMSO, London.

Home Office/DoH (1992) *Memorandum of Good Practice*, HMSO, London.

Home Office, DoH, DES and Welsh Office (1991) *Working Together*, HMSO, London.

House of Commons (1985) *Community Care, Social Services Committee 2nd Report, Session 1984–5*, Vol. 1, HC13–1.

House of Commons (1990) *Annual Report of the Data Protection Registrar, Home Affairs Committee 1st Report, Session 1990–1*, HC115.

House of Commons (1991) *Protection of individuals in relation to processing of personal data in the community and information security*, Document No. 8460/90, European Standing Committee B, 5 June.

House of Commons (1993) *Juvenile Offenders Vol. 1, 6th Report of the Home Affairs Committee, Session 1992–3*, HC441–1.

House of Lords (1993) *Protection of Personal Data, Select Committee on the European Communities 20th Report, Session 1992–3*, HL75.

Howard League (1985) *Unlawful Sex*, Waterlow, London.

Hughes, B. and Parker, H. (1994) 'Save the Children', *Community Care*, 3 March.

Hyder, K. and Rose, D. (1994) 'Police demand their "FBI" to fend off MI5', *Observer*, 13 November.

Ignatieff, M. (1978) *A Just Measure of Pain*, Random House, New York.

Johnson, D. (1989) 'Beverley case fuels pressure to close loopholes in care', *Guardian*, 2 November.

Jones, G. (1994) 'Major backs ID cards to fight crime', *Daily Telegraph*, 8 June.

Jones, R. (1994) *Mental Health Act Manual* (4th edn), Sweet and Maxwell, London.

JUSTICE (1970) *Privacy and the Law*, Stevens and Sons, London.

Kagle, J.D. (1991) *Social Work Records* (2nd edn), Wadsworth, California.

Kimball, P. (1984) *The File*, George Allen and Unwin, London.

King's Fund Centre (1991) *Counselling for Regulated Infertility Treatments*, King's Fund Centre, London.

Kinnibrugh, A.D. (1984) *Social work case recording and the client's right to privacy*, Occasional Paper No. 12, School of advanced Urban Studies, University of Bristol.

Langdale, R. and Maskrey S. (1994) 'Public interest immunity: Disclosure of social work records', *Family Law*, September, Vol. 24, pp. 513–16.

Law Commission (1981) *Breach of Confidence*, Report No. 110, Cmnd 8388, HMSO, London.

Law Commission (1993) *Mentally Incapacitated Adults and Other Vulnerable Adults: Public Law Protection*, Consultation Paper No. 130, HMSO, London.

Leicestershire County Council (1980) *Carly Taylor: Report of an Independent Inquiry*, Leicestershire County Council, Leicester.

Levy, A. and Kahan, B. (1991) *The Pindown Experience and the Protection of Children*, Staffordshire County Council, Stoke-on-Trent.

Liberty (1993) *A right to be left alone? Liberty's response to the government's consultation paper, infringement of privacy*, Liberty, London, October.

Liberty (1994a) *Sexuality and the State: Report No. 6*, Liberty, London.

Liberty (1994b) *Censored: Freedom of expression and human rights*, Liberty, London.

Lightfoot, L. (1994) 'Child Specialist in new abuse scandal', *The Sunday Times*, 20 November.

Lilley, J.R. (1990) 'Tagging Reviewed', *The Howard Journal of Criminal Justice*, Vol. 29, No. 4, pp. 229–45.

Lindop, N. (1983) 'Data Protection: The Background', in Bourn and Benyon (1983).

Lindop Report (1978) *Report of the Committee on Data Protection*, Cmnd 7341, HMSO, London.

Littlechild, B. (1994) *The Social Worker as Appropriate Adult under the Police and Criminal Evidence Act 1984*, BASW, London.

London Borough of Brent (1985) *A Child in Trust: The Report of the Panel of Inquiry into the Circumstances Surrounding the Death of Jasmine Beckford*, London Borough of Brent, London.

London Borough of Greenwich (1987) *A Child in Mind: Protection of Children in a Responsible Society*, London Borough of Greenwich, London.

London Borough of Hillingdon Area Review Committee (1986) *Report of the Review Panel into the Death of Heidi Koseda*, London Borough of Hillingdon, Uxbridge.

London Borough of Lambeth (1987) *Whose Child?: The Report of the Public Inquiry into the Death of Tyra Henry*, London Borough of Lambeth, Brixton.

Lord Chancellor's Department (1993) *Infringement of Privacy*, Lord Chancellor's Department, London, July.

Lyon, D. (1991) 'British Identity Cards: The Unpalatable Logic of European Membership?' *The Political Quarterly*, No. 6293 July–September.

Lyon, D. (1994) *The Electronic Eye*, Polity Press, Cambridge.

MacVeigh, J. (1982) *Gaskin*, Jonathan Cape, London.

Maguire, S. (1988) '"Sorry love" – violence against women in the home and the state response', *Critical Social Policy*, No. 23, pp. 34–45.

Margolin, L. (1992) 'Deviance on record: Techniques for labelling child abusers in official documents', *Social Problems*, Vol. 39, No. 1, February, pp. 58–70.

McShane, R., Hope, T. and Wilkinson, J. (1994) 'Tracking patients who wander: Ethics and technology', *The Lancet*, 21 May, p. 1,274.

McWilliams, W. and Pease, K. (1990) 'Probation practice and an end to Punishment', *Howard Journal of Criminal Justice*, Vol. 29, No. 1, pp. 14–24.

Metropolitan Police and Bexley Social Services (1987) *Child Sexual Abuse: Joint investigative programme – Final Report*, HMSO, London.

Michael, J. (1994) *Privacy and Human Rights*, Dartmouth/UNESCO, Aldershot/Paris.

MIND (1994a) 'Health chiefs should spend £77 million on community care not "illegal" supervision registers' (press release), 14 July.

MIND (1994b) *MIND's Response to the Department of Health's Guidance on Supervision Registers and on Hospital Discharge*, MIND, London, 6 July.

Ministry of Health (1959) *Social workers in the local authority health and welfare services*, HMSO, London.

Morgan, B. (1994) 'Child Abuse Challenge', *Times Higher Education Supplement*, 10 June.

Morris, A., Giller, H., Szwed, E. and Geach, H. (1980) *Justice for Children*, Macmillan, London.

Morris, B. (1987) 'Keys to the Future', *Social Services Insight*, 18 September.

Murray, N. (1993) 'Legal Clout', *Community Care*, 1 July, pp. 16–17.

NCCL (1988) *Identity cards and the threat to civil liberties*, Civil Liberty Briefing No. 12, NCCL, London.

NCIS (National Criminal Intelligence Service) (1994) 'National Criminal Intelligence Service reshapes itself' (press release), 14 June.

NE Thames and SE Thames Regional Health Authorities (1994) *The Report of the Inquiry into the Care and Treatment of Christopher Clunis*, HMSO, London.

Neate, P. (1990) 'Sinister Forces', *Community Care*, 31 May.

Nellis, M. (1991) 'The Electronic Monitoring of Offenders in England and Wales', *British Journal of Criminology*, Vol. 31, No. 2, pp. 165–85.

Neville, D. and Beak, D. (1990) 'Solving the case history mystery', *Social Work Today*, 28 June.

Newell, P. (1991) *The U.N. Convention and Children's Rights in the UK*, National Children's Bureau, London.

NHS Management Executive (1991) *Access to Health Records Act 1990*, NHS Management Executive, Leeds.

NHS Management Executive (1994) *Introduction of supervision registers for mentally ill people from 1 April 1994*, February, reference HSG(94)5.

No Turning Back Group (1993) *Who Benefits? Re-inventing Social Security*, NTBG, London, August.

Norris, D. (1990) *Violence against Social Workers*, Jessica Kingsley, London.

OECD (Organisation for Economic Co-operation and Development) (1980) *Guidelines on the Protection of Privacy and Transborder flows of Personal Data*, OECD, Paris.

OECD (Organisation for Economic Co-operation and Development) (1994) *Privacy and Data Protection: Issues and Challenges*, OECD, Paris.

Official Solicitor (1988) *The Cleveland Child Abuse Inquiry: The Investigations and Submissions of the Official Solicitor to the Supreme Court.*

Ogden, J. (1992) 'Murder report leads to guidance call', *Social Work Today*, 11 June.

Orwell, G. (1949) *Nineteen Eighty-Four*, Secker and Warburg, London.

Oulton, C. (1990) 'Hoaxers may be child abuse vigilantes', *The Independent on Sunday*, 20 May.

Ovretveit, J. (1985) *Client access and social work recording*, BASW, London.

Ovretveit, J. (1986) *Improving Social Work Records and Practice*, BASW, London.

Page, R. and Clark, G.A. (eds) (1977) *Who Cares?*, National Children's Bureau, London.

Parker, R. (1990) *Safeguarding Standards*, NISW, London.

Parry, A. (1985) 'Just Good Practice?', *Community Care*, 24 October.

Parton, N. (1991) *Governing the family*, Macmillan, Basingstoke.

Payne, M. (1989) 'Open Records and Shared Decisions with Clients', in Shardlow (1989).

Pearce, P., Parsloe, P., Francis, H., Macara, A. and Watson, D. (1988) *Personal Data Protection in Health and Social Services*, Croom Helm, London.

Pickford, R. (1992) 'The Gaskin case and Confidential Personal Information', *Journal of Child Law*, Vol. 4, No. 1, pp. 33–8.

Pidgeon, J. and Bates, P. (1990) 'Intervention: Protection or control?', *Social Work Today*, 11 January.

Pithouse, A. (1990) 'Guardians of autonomy: Work orientations in a social work office', in Carter et al. (1990).

Powell, F. (1980) 'Is Big Brother Watching You?', *Social Work Today*, 24 June.

Raab, C.D. (1993) 'Data protection in Britain: Governance and Learning', *Governance*, Vol. 6, No. 1, January, pp. 43–66.

Raab, C.D. and Bennett, C. (1994) 'Protecting privacy across borders: European policies and prospects', *Public Administration*, Vol. 72, No. 1, Spring, pp. 95–112.

Radzinowicz, L. and Hood, R. (1990) *The Emergence of Penal Policy in Victorian and Edwardian England*, Clarendon Press, Oxford.

RCCJ (Royal Commission on Criminal Justice) (1993) Cm 2263, HMSO, London.

RCN (Royal College of Nursing) (1994) *The Privacy of Clients: Electronic tagging and closed circuit television*, RCN, London, March.

Rojek, C., Peacock, G. and Collins, S. (1988) *Social Work and Received Ideas*, Routledge, London.

Rule, J. (1973) *Private Lives and Public Surveillance*, Allen Lane, London.

Sampson, A. (1994) *Acts of Abuse: Sex Offenders and the Criminal Justice System*, Routledge, London.

Satyamurti, C. (1981) *Occupational Survival*, Blackwells, Oxford.

Sayce, L. (1991) 'Registering – A risky business?', *Social Work Today*, 4 July.

SCA (Social Care Association) (1988) *Code of Practice for Social Care*, SCA, Surbiton.

Schutte, P. (1989) 'Medical confidentiality and a police murder inquiry', *Journal of the Medical Defence Union*, No. 5, Spring.

Scottish Education Department (1989a) *Code on Confidentiality of Social Work Records*, Social Work Services Group Circular SWI/1989.

Scottish Education Department (1989b) *Access to Personal Files (Social Work) (Scotland) Regulation 1989*, Social Work Services Group Circular SCS2/89.

Seebohm Report (1968) *Report of the Committee on Local Authority and Allied Personal Social Services*, Cmnd 3703, HMSO, London.

Sennett, R. (1977) *The Fall of Public Man*, Cambridge University Press, Cambridge.

Shardlow, S. (ed.) (1989) *The Values of Change in Social Work*, Tavistock/Routledge, London.

Shemmings, D. (1991) *Client Access to Records: Participation in Social Work*, Avebury, Aldershot.

Sieghart, P. (1983) 'Information privacy and the Data Protection Bill', in Bourn and Benyon (1983).

Simpkin, M. (1989) 'Holistic Health Care and Professional Values', in Shardlow (1989).

Sparks, R. (1992) *Television and the drama of Crime: Moral tales and the place of crime in public life*, Open University Press, Buckingham.

SSI (Social Services Inspectorate) (1990) *Guidance on Standards for Residential Homes for Elderly People*, HMSO, London.

SSI (Social Services Inspectorate) (1991a) *Care Management and Assessment: Managers' Guide*, Department of Health, London.

SSI (Social Services Inspectorate) (1991b) *Assessment Systems and Community Care*, Department of Health, London.

SSI (Social Services Inspectorate) (1991c) *Care Management and Assessment: Practitioners' Guide*, Department of Health, London.

SSI (Social Services Inspectorate) (1991d) *Getting the Message Across*, HMSO, London.

SSI (Social Services Inspectorate) (1993a) *Inspection of Residential Child Care Services: Calderdale Social Services Department*, Department of Health, London.

SSI (Social Services Inspectorate) (1993b) *Corporate Parents*, Department of Health, London.

SSI (Social Services Inspectorate) (1993c) *Community Care*, SSI letter EL(93)119, 23 December, Department of Health, London, para. 9.

SSI (Social Services Inspectorate) (1994a) *Putting People First – The Third Annual Report of the Chief Inspector, Social Services Inspectorate 1993–4*, Department of Health, London.

SSI (Social Services Inspectorate) (1994b) *Inspection of Local Authority Services for People Affected by HIV/AIDS: Overview*, Department of Health, London.

SSI (Social Services Inspectorate) (1994c) *Inspecting Social Services: Practice Guidance*, Department of Health, London, April.

SSI (Social Services Inspectorate) (1994d) *Evaluating child protection services: Findings and issues*, Department of Health, London.

SSI (NI) (Social Services Inspectorate (Northern Ireland)) (1991) *People First: Care Management – Guidance on assessment and the provision of community care*, Department of Health and Social Services, Belfast.

Staffordshire Area Child Protection Committee (1994) *Guidelines for the multi-agency management of patients suspected or at risk of suffering from life-threatening abuse resulting in cyanotic-apnoeic episodes*.

Staffordshire Police (1993) 'Working together to beat truancy' (press release), 22 September.

Stallworthy, M. (1990) 'Data Protection: Regulation in a Deregulatory State', *Statute Law Review*, Vol. 11, No. 2, pp. 130–54.

Stockford, D. (ed.) (1988) *Integrating Care Systems: Practical perspectives*, Longman, Harlow.

Stone, R.T.H. (1989) *Entry, Search and Seizure: A Guide to Civil and Criminal Powers of Entry* (2nd edn), Sweet and Maxwell, London.

Sutton, D. (1991) 'A Betrayal of trust', *Community Care*, 23 May.

Thomas, T. (1994a) *The Police and Social Workers* (2nd edn), Arena, Aldershot.

Thomas, T. (1994b) 'Covert Video Surveillance', *New Law Journal*, 15 July, Vol. 144, No. 6656, pp. 966–7.

Thomas, T. (1994c) 'Covert Video Surveillance in Child Protection Work', *Family Law*, September, Vol. 24, pp. 524–6.

Thompson, I.E. (1979) 'The nature of confidentiality', *Journal of Medical Ethics*, No. 5, pp. 57–64.

Thorpe, D.H., Smith, D., Green, C.J. and Paley, J.H. (1980) *Out of Care: The community support of juvenile offenders*, George Allen and Unwin, London.

Timms, N. (1972) *Recording in Social Work*, RKP, London.

Travis, A. (1990) 'Police to set up register for women at risk of home violence', *Guardian*, 18 May.

Tregaskis, B. and Mayberry, J.F. (1994) 'The Anniversary of Section 47 of the National Assistance Act 1948', *Justice of the Peace and Local Government Law*, 23 April, Vol. 158, No. 17.

Turl, P. (1994) '"Stalking" is a public problem', *New Law Journal*, 12 May, Vol. 144, No. 6647, pp. 632–3.

Turnbull, G. (1986) *Information Technology and Social Work*, University of East Anglia/*Social Work Today*, Monograph No. 43.

United Nations (1948) *Universal Declaration of Human Rights*, United Nations, New York.

United Nations (1989) *Convention on the Rights of the Child*, United Nations, New York.

Violence against Children Study Group (1990) *Taking Child Abuse Seriously*, Unwin Hyman, London.

Wacks, R. (1989) *Personal Information*, Clarendon Press, Oxford.

Wagner Report (1988) *Residential Care: A positive choice*, HMSO, London.

Ward, S. (1993) 'Adoptive parents sue over boy's "hidden" past', *The Independent*, 22 February.

Warren, S.D. and Brandeis, I.D. (1890) 'The right to privacy', Vol. 4, *Harvard Law Review*, p. 193.

Watts, S. (1994) 'Computer data watchdog "ineffective and costly"', *The Independent*, 6 July.

West Yorkshire Police (1992) *West Yorkshire Chief Constable's Annual Report*.

Westin, A. (1967) *Privacy and Freedom*, Bodley Head, London.

White, R. (1992) 'Confidentiality and Privilege: Child Abuse and Child Abduction', *Child Abuse Review*, No. 1, pp. 60–4.

Working Mothers Association (1992) *Day Care in the Home*, WMA, London.

Wright, P. (1987) *Spycatcher*, Viking, New York.

Younger Report (1972) *Report of the Committee on Privacy*, Cmnd 5012, HMSO, London.

Zuckerman, A.S.S. (1990) 'The Weakness of the PACE Special Procedure for Protecting Confidential Material', *Criminal Law Review*, July, pp. 472–8.

Index

absconders 31, 108–9
access to files 38, 40, 76, 79, 91–103
Access to Health Records Act (1990) 103
Access to Medical Records Act (1990) 103
Access to Personal Files Act (1987) 69,
    96, 97–102
Administration of Justice Act (1960)
    109–110
Administration of Justice Act (1970) 93
adoption 61, 79, 81, 85
Adoption Act (1976) 100
advocacy 69
appropriate adult 117–18
Association of Directors of Social
    Services (ADSS) 108
audio tapes 50, 101
Audit Commission 121
Austria 10

Barclay Report 29
Barnsley 70
Beckford, Jasmine 39
Belgium 10
Bentham, Jeremy 3
Birmingham 79
bogus social workers 21–2
breach of confidence 75
British Association of Social Workers
    (BASW) 22, 28, 39, 40–43, 55, 63,
    77, 79, 82, 93, 102, 124, 128
British Medical Association (BMA) 68
Brown, Paul 39
Bulger, James 108, 126

bureaucracy 5–6, 8

Calcutt Report 11, 15, 108
Cambridgeshire 30
Campaign for Freedom of Information
    95–6
Carlile, Kimberley 24
case file 5, 37–8, 40–45
cautioning young offenders 107
Charity Organisations Society (COS) 5,
    37–8
Child Assessment Order 42, 115
child protection 19, 23–5, 31, 42, 47, 51,
    52, 105
child protection conferences 42–3, 114–
    15
Child Protection Register 45–7, 50, 71,
    87, 113, 115
Childline 32
childminders 47, 81
Children Act (1989) 21, 24–6, 32–3, 43,
    46, 47, 48, 69, 72, 78, 79, 109, 114,
    115
Children and Young Persons Act (1933)
    25, 47, 107, 116
Children and Young Persons Act (1969)
    118
children's homes 30–31, 54
    permissable forms of control 31–2
    telephones 32–3
Children's Legal Centre 32–3, 59, 94
Chronically Sick and Disabled Persons
    Act (1970) 48

145

The Police and Social Workers

Second Edition

Terry Thomas

Social workers and police officers are in daily contact with one another in various areas of their work. This book offers a clear guide to that inter-agency work and critically examines how it is carried out in practice.

This second edition of the book has been substantially revised to take account of changes in the law, policy and procedures affecting both police and social workers. In particular the Children Act 1989, The Criminal Justice Act 1991 and the findings of the Royal Commission on Criminal Justice 1993. The opportunity has also been taken to revise parts of the original text to ensure as clear a light as possible is thrown on police-social work collaboration – illustrating both the positive and the negative.

Terry Thomas is Senior Lecturer in Social Work at Leeds Metropolitan University.

1994   346 pages   1 85742 157 4   £14.95

Price subject to change without notification

Advocacy Skills

A HANDBOOK FOR HUMAN SERVICE PROFESSIONALS

Neil Bateman

Advocacy is a skill used by many people in human service organisations. Social workers, community medical staff and advice workers are a few who will use such skills. Advocacy is used to overcome obstacles and to secure tangible results for customers – extra money, better services and housing. Neil Bateman's book sets out a model for effective professional practice, and outlines a number of approaches to advocacy.

This is a seminal work; no other book has been published in the UK which explains how advocacy skills can be used and developed. Advocacy is becoming part of the everyday work of many people. Advocacy Skills will be a valuable handbook for anyone concerned with the rights of others.

Neil Bateman is currently a Principal Officer with Suffolk County Council, an adviser to the Association of County Councils and a visiting lecturer at the University of East Anglia.

1995   176 pages   1 85742 200 7   £14.95

Price subject to change without notification

arena